AA004076

CLOUD COMPUTING 2021

The Twelfth International Conference on Cloud Computing, GRIDs, and Virtualization

April 18 - 22, 2021

CLOUD COMPUTING 2021 Editors

Bob Duncan, University of Aberdeen, UK
Yong Woo Lee, University of Seoul, South Korea
Manuela Popescu, IARIA, EU/USA

Printed from e-media with permission by:

Curran Associates, Inc.
57 Morehouse Lane
Red Hook, NY 12571

Some format issues inherent in the e-media version may also appear in this print version.

Copyright© (2021) by International Academy, Research, and Industry Association (IARIA)
Please refer to the Copyright Information page.

Printed with permission by Curran Associates, Inc. (2023)

International Academy, Research, and Industry Association (IARIA)
412 Derby Way
Wilmington, DE 19810

Phone: (408) 893-6407
Fax: (408) 527-6351

petre@iaria.org

Additional copies of this publication are available from:

Curran Associates, Inc.
57 Morehouse Lane
Red Hook, NY 12571 USA
Phone: 845-758-0400
Fax: 845-758-2633
Email: curran@proceedings.com
Web: www.proceedings.com

Table of Contents

CLOUD COMPUTING 2021

Forward

The Twelfth International Conference on Cloud Computing, GRIDs, and Virtualization (CLOUD COMPUTING 2021), held on April 18 - 22, 2021, continued a series of events targeted to prospect the applications supported by the new paradigm and validate the techniques and the mechanisms. A complementary target was to identify the open issues and the challenges to fix them, especially on security, privacy, and inter- and intra-clouds protocols.

Cloud computing is a normal evolution of distributed computing combined with Service-oriented architecture, leveraging most of the GRID features and Virtualization merits. The technology foundations for cloud computing led to a new approach of reusing what was achieved in GRID computing with support from virtualization.

The conference had the following tracks:

- Cloud computing
- Computing in virtualization-based environments
- Platforms, infrastructures and applications
- Challenging features

Similar to the previous edition, this event attracted excellent contributions and active participation from all over the world. We were very pleased to receive top quality contributions.

We take here the opportunity to warmly thank all the members of the CLOUD COMPUTING 2021 technical program committee, as well as the numerous reviewers. The creation of such a high quality conference program would not have been possible without their involvement. We also kindly thank all the authors that dedicated much of their time and effort to contribute to CLOUD COMPUTING 2021. We truly believe that, thanks to all these efforts, the final conference program consisted of top quality contributions.

Also, this event could not have been a reality without the support of many individuals, organizations and sponsors. We also gratefully thank the members of the CLOUD COMPUTING 2021 organizing committee for their help in handling the logistics and for their work that made this professional meeting a success.

We hope that CLOUD COMPUTING 2021 was a successful international forum for the exchange of ideas and results between academia and industry and to promote further progress in the area of cloud computing, GRIDs and virtualization.

CLOUD COMPUTING 2021 Steering Committee

Carlos Becker Westphall, Federal University of Santa Catarina, Brazil
Yong Woo Lee, University of Seoul, Korea
Bob Duncan, University of Aberdeen, UK

Aspen Olmsted, College of Charleston, USA
Alex Sim, Lawrence Berkeley National Laboratory, USA
Sören Frey, Daimler TSS GmbH, Germany
Andreas Aßmuth, Ostbayerische Technische Hochschule (OTH) Amberg-Weiden, Germany
Uwe Hohenstein, Siemens AG, Germany
Magnus Westerlund, Arcada, Finland

CLOUD COMPUTING 2021 Publicity Chair

Jose Luis García, Universitat Politecnica de Valencia, Spain
Lorena Parra, Universitat Politecnica de Valencia, Spain

CLOUD COMPUTING 2021 Industry/Research Advisory Committee

Raul Valin Ferreiro, Fujitsu Laboratories of Europe, Spain
Bill Karakostas, VLTN gcv, Antwerp, Belgium
Matthias Olzmann, noventum consulting GmbH - Münster, Germany
Hong Zhu, Oxford Brookes University, UK

CLOUD COMPUTING 2021

Committee

CLOUD COMPUTING 2021 Steering Committee

Carlos Becker Westphall, Federal University of Santa Catarina, Brazil
Yong Woo Lee, University of Seoul, Korea
Bob Duncan, University of Aberdeen, UK
Aspen Olmsted, College of Charleston, USA
Alex Sim, Lawrence Berkeley National Laboratory, USA
Sören Frey, Daimler TSS GmbH, Germany
Andreas Aßmuth, Ostbayerische Technische Hochschule (OTH) Amberg-Weiden, Germany
Uwe Hohenstein, Siemens AG, Germany
Magnus Westerlund, Arcada, Finland

CLOUD COMPUTING 2021 Industry/Research Advisory Committee

Raul Valin Ferreiro, Fujitsu Laboratories of Europe, Spain
Bill Karakostas, VLTN gcv, Antwerp, Belgium
Matthias Olzmann, noventum consulting GmbH - Münster, Germany
Hong Zhu, Oxford Brookes University, UK

CLOUD COMPUTING 2021 Publicity Chairs

Jose Luis García, Universitat Politecnica de Valencia, Spain
Lorena Parra, Universitat Politecnica de Valencia, Spain

CLOUD COMPUTING 2021 Technical Program Committee

Sherif Abdelwahed, Virginia Commonwealth University, USA
Maruf Ahmed, The University of Technology, Sydney, Australia
Abdulelah Alwabel, Prince Sattam Bin Abdulaziz University, Kingdom of Saudi Arabia
Mário Antunes, Polytechnic of Leiria, Portugal
Ali Anwar, IBM Research, USA
Filipe Araujo, University of Coimbra, Portugal
Andreas Aßmuth, Ostbayerische Technische Hochschule (OTH) Amberg-Weiden, Germany
Odiljon Atabaev, Andijan Machine-Building Institute, Uzbekistan
Luis-Eduardo Bautista-Villalpando, Autonomous University of Aguascalientes, Mexico
Carlos Becker Westphall, Federal University of Santa Catarina, Brazil
Andreas Berl, Technische Hochschule Deggendorf, Germany
Simona Bernardi, University of Zaragoza, Spain
Dixit Bhatta, University of Delaware, USA
Anirban Bhattacharjee, National Institute of Standards and Technology (NIST), USA

Peter Bloodsworth, University of Oxford, UK
Jalil Boukhobza, University of Western Brittany, France
Marco Brocanelli, Wayne State University, USA
Antonio Brogi, University of Pisa, Italy
Roberta Calegari, Alma Mater Studiorum-Università di Bologna, Italy
Paolo Campegiani, Bit4id, Italy
Juan Vicente Capella Hernández, Universitat Politècnica de València, Spain
Roberto Casadei, Alma Mater Studiorum - Università di Bologna, Italy
Ruay-Shiung Chang, National Taipei University of Business, Taipei, Taiwan
Yue Cheng, George Mason University, USA
Ryan Chard, Argonne National Laboratory, USA
Batyr Charyyev, Stevens Institute of Technology, USA
Hao Che, University of Texas at Arlington, USA
Enrique Chirivella Perez, University West of Scotland, UK
Claudio Cicconetti, National Research Council, Italy
Daniel Corujo, Universidade de Aveiro | Instituto de Telecomunicações, Portugal
Noel De Palma, University Grenoble Alpes, France
Mª del Carmen Carrión Espinosa, University of Castilla-La Mancha, Spain
Chen Ding, Ryerson University, Canada
Ramon dos Reis Fontes, Federal University of Rio Grande do Norte, Natal, Brazil
Bob Duncan, University of Aberdeen, UK
Steve Eager, University West of Scotland, UK
Nabil El Ioini, Free University of Bolzano, Italy
Rania Fahim El-Gazzar, Universty of South-Eastern Norway, Norway
Ibrahim El-Shekeil, Metropolitan State University, USA
Levent Ertaul, California State University, East Bay, USA
Javier Fabra, Universidad de Zaragoza, Spain
Fairouz Fakhfakh, University of Sfax, Tunisia
Umar Farooq, University of California, Riverside, USA
Tadeu Ferreira Oliveira, Federal Institute of Science Education and Technology of Rio Grande do Norte, Brazil
Jan Fesl, Institute of Applied Informatics - University of South Bohemia, Czech Republic
Sebastian Fischer, OTH Regensburg, Germany
Stefano Forti, University of Pisa, Italy
Sören Frey, Daimler TSS GmbH, Germany
Somchart Fugkeaw, Sirindhorn International Institute of Technology | Thammasat University, Thailand
Juan Fumero, University of Manchester, UK
Katja Gilly, Miguel Hernandez University, Spain
Jing Gong, KTH, Sweden
Poonam Goyal, Birla Institute of Technology & Science, Pilani, India
Nils Gruschka, University of Oslo, Norway
Jordi Guitart, Universitat Politècnica de Catalunya - Barcelona Supercomputing Center, Spain
Saurabh Gupta, Graphic Era Deemed to be University, Dehradun, India
Seif Haridi, KTH/SICS, Sweden
Herodotos Herodotou, Cyprus University of Technology, Cyprus
Uwe Hohenstein, Siemens AG Munich, Germany
Soamar Homsi, Air Force Research Laboratory (AFRL), USA
Anca Daniela Ionita, University Politehnica of Bucharest, Romania

Saba Jamalian, Roosevelt University / Braze, USA
Fuad Jamour, University of California, Riverside, USA
Vitor Jesus, Birmingham City University, UK
Weiwei Jia, New Jersey Institute of Technology, USA
Carlos Juiz, University of the Balearic Islands, Spain
Bill Karakostas, VLTN gcv, Antwerp, Belgium
Sokratis Katsikas, Norwegian University of Science and Technology, Norway
Attila Kertesz, University of Szeged, Hungary
Zaheer Khan, University of the West of England, Bristol, UK
Ioannis Konstantinou, CSLAB - NTUA, Greece
Sonal Kumari, Samsung R&D Institute, India
Van Thanh Le, Free University of Bozen-Bolzano, Italy
Yong Woo Lee, University of Seoul, Korea
Sarah Lehman, Temple University, USA
Kunal Lillaney, Amazon Web Services, USA
Yuhui Lin, University of St Andrews, UK
Panos Linos, Butler University, USA
Enjie Liu, University of Bedfordshire, UK
Xiaodong Liu, Edinburgh Napier University, UK
Jay Lofstead, Sandia National Laboratories, USA
Hui Lu, Binghamton University (State University of New York), USA
Weibin Ma, University of Delaware, USA
Hosein Mohammadi Makrani, University of California, Davis, USA
Shaghayegh Mardani, University of California Los Angeles (UCLA), USA
Stefano Mariani, University of Modena and Reggio Emilia, Italy
Attila Csaba Marosi, Institute for Computer Science and Control - Hungarian Academy of Sciences, Hungary
Romolo Marotta, University of l'Aquila (UNIVAQ), Italy
Antonio Matencio Escolar, University West of Scotland, UK
Jean-Marc Menaud, IMT Atlantique, France
Philippe Merle, Inria, France
Nasro Min-Allah, Imam Abdulrahman Bin Faisal University (IAU), KSA
Preeti Mishra, Graphic Era Deemed to be University, Dehradun, India
Francesc D. Muñoz-Escoí, Universitat Politècnica de València, Spain
Ioannis Mytilinis, National Technical University of Athens, Greece
Antonio Nehme, Birmingham City University, UK
Hidemoto Nakada, National Institute of Advanced Industrial Science and Technology (AIST), Japan
Richard Neill, RN Technologies LLC, USA
Marco Netto, IBM Research, Brazil
Jens Nicolay, Vrije Universiteit Brussel, Belgium
Ridwan Rashid Noel, Texas Lutheran University, USA
Alexander Norta, Tallinn Technology University, Estonia
Aspen Olmsted, College of Charleston, USA
Matthias Olzmann, noventum consulting GmbH - Münster, Germany
Brajendra Panda, University of Arkansas, USA
Lorena Parra, Universitat Politècnica de València, Spain
Arnab K. Paul, Oak Ridge National Laboratory, USA
Alessandro Pellegrini, National Research Council (CNR), Italy

Tamas Pflanzner, University of Szeged, Hungary
Paulo Pires, Fluminense Federal University (UFF), Brazil
Agostino Poggi, Università degli Studi di Parma, Italy
Walter Priesnitz Filho, Federal University of Santa Maria, Rio Grande do Sul, Brazil
Abena Primo, Huston-Tillotson University, USA
Mohammed A Qadeer, Aligarh Muslim University, India
Francesco Quaglia, University of Rome Tor Vergata, Italy
M. Mustafa Rafique, Rochester Institute of Technology, USA
Danda B. Rawat, Howard University, USA
Daniel A. Reed, University of Utah, USA
Christoph Reich, Hochschule Furtwangen University, Germany
Eduard Gibert Renart, Rutgers Unversity, USA
Ruben Ricart Sanchez, University West of Scotland, UK
Sashko Ristov, University of Innsbruck, Austria
Javier Rocher Morant, Universitat Politecnica de Valencia, Spain
Ivan Rodero, Rutgers University, USA
Takfarinas Saber, University College Dublin, Ireland
Hemanta Sapkota, University of Nevada - Reno, USA
Lutz Schubert, University of Ulm, Germany
Savio Sciancalepore, TU Eindhoven, Netherlands
Wael Sellami, Higher Institute of Computer Sciences of Mahdia - ReDCAD laboratory, Tunisia
Jianchen Shan, Hofstra University, USA
Muhammad Abu Bakar Siddique, University of California, Riverside, USA
Altino Manuel Silva Sampaio, Escola Superior de Tecnologia e Gestão | Instituto Politécnico do Porto, Portugal
Alex Sim, Lawrence Berkeley National Laboratory, USA
Soeren Sonntag, Intel, Germany
Vasily Tarasov, IBM Research, USA
Bedir Tekinerdogan, Wageningen University, The Netherlands
Prashanth Thinakaran, Pennsylvania StateUniversity / Adobe Research, USA
Orazio Tomarchio, University of Catania, Italy
Reza Tourani, Saint Louis University, USA
Raul Valin Ferreiro, Fujitsu Laboratories of Europe, Spain
AntonioVirdis, University of Pisa, Italy
Massimo Villari, Università di Messina, Italy
Teng Wang, Oracle, USA
Hironori Washizaki, Waseda University, Japan
Mandy Weißbach, Martin Luther University of Halle-Wittenberg, Germany
Magnus Westerlund, Arcada, Finland
Liuqing Yang, Columbia University in the City of New York, USA
Christos Zaroliagis, CTI & University of Patras, Greece
Ahmed Zekri, Beirut Arab University, Lebanon
Zhiming Zhao, University of Amsterdam, Netherlands
Jiang Zhou, Institute of Information Engineering - Chinese Academy of Sciences, China
Hong Zhu, Oxford Brookes University, UK
Jan Henrik Ziegeldorf, RWTH Aachen University, Germany
Wolf Zimmermann, Martin Luther University Halle-Wittenberg, Germany

Markus Zoppelt, Nuremberg Institute of Technology (TH Nürnberg) / Friedrich-Alexander-Universität Erlangen Nürnberg (FAU), Germany

Copyright Information

For your reference, this is the text governing the copyright release for material published by IARIA.

The copyright release is a transfer of publication rights, which allows IARIA and its partners to drive the dissemination of the published material. This allows IARIA to give articles increased visibility via distribution, inclusion in libraries, and arrangements for submission to indexes.

I, the undersigned, declare that the article is original, and that I represent the authors of this article in the copyright release matters. If this work has been done as work-for-hire, I have obtained all necessary clearances to execute a copyright release. I hereby irrevocably transfer exclusive copyright for this material to IARIA. I give IARIA permission or reproduce the work in any media format such as, but not limited to, print, digital, or electronic. I give IARIA permission to distribute the materials without restriction to any institutions or individuals. I give IARIA permission to submit the work for inclusion in article repositories as IARIA sees fit.

I, the undersigned, declare that to the best of my knowledge, the article is does not contain libelous or otherwise unlawful contents or invading the right of privacy or infringing on a proprietary right.

Following the copyright release, any circulated version of the article must bear the copyright notice and any header and footer information that IARIA applies to the published article.

IARIA grants royalty-free permission to the authors to disseminate the work, under the above provisions, for any academic, commercial, or industrial use. IARIA grants royalty-free permission to any individuals or institutions to make the article available electronically, online, or in print.

IARIA acknowledges that rights to any algorithm, process, procedure, apparatus, or articles of manufacture remain with the authors and their employers.

I, the undersigned, understand that IARIA will not be liable, in contract, tort (including, without limitation, negligence), pre-contract or other representations (other than fraudulent misrepresentations) or otherwise in connection with the publication of my work.

Exception to the above is made for work-for-hire performed while employed by the government. In that case, copyright to the material remains with the said government. The rightful owners (authors and government entity) grant unlimited and unrestricted permission to IARIA, IARIA's contractors, and IARIA's partners to further distribute the work.

IT Security of Cloud Services and IoT Devices in Healthcare

Michael Gleißner[1,2], Johannes Dotzler[1], Juliana Hartig[1], Andreas Aßmuth[2], Clemens Bulitta[1] and Steffen Hamm[1]

Technical University of Applied Sciences OTH Amberg-Weiden
[1] Hetzenrichter Weg 15, 92637 Weiden, Germany
[2] Kaiser-Wilhelm-Ring 23, 92224 Amberg, Germany

email: {m.gleissner | jo.dotzler | j.hartig | a.assmuth | c.bulitta | s.hamm}@oth-aw.de

Abstract—**The continuous evolution of new technologies is going to rapidly transform several sectors. A widespread hypothesis claims that especially the healthcare sector will undergo a drastic transformation with the integration of medical Internet of Things (IoT) devices. The use of medical IoT devices results in the implementation of necessary medically approved hardware, software and attached cloud services. This leads to new Information Technology (IT) security challenges and demands for new IT security concepts. This paper aims to identify upcoming security challenges by researching existing IT security guidelines targeting network-connected medical IoT devices, their users and the attached cloud services in homecare and integrated care.**

Keywords*—*Internet of Things; healthcare; medical IoT; cloud services.

I. Introduction

According to the Check Point Software Technologies Ltd. Security Report from 2020, more than 90 percent of companies use cloud services, with 67 percent of security departments complaining about a lack of transparency in their cloud infrastructure and compliance. The number of attacks on cloud services has increased in 2019 and is expected to continue rising in the following years. Above all, the incorrect configuration of cloud systems is identified to be a major problem [1]. Additionally, the number of active connections to the Internet of Things (IoT) will grow worldwide from 8.74 million in 2020 to 25.44 million in 2030 [2].

The benefits of more devices and cloud services will ensure a high potential for innovation especially in the healthcare sector. However, this also increases the risk of attacks. The healthcare sector is an area where particularly sensitive information is stored and processed. In this field, digitization is seen as a key factor for growth and the opportunity for modernization. Although Germany only ranks second to last when it comes to digitization in the healthcare system compared to other European countries, there is a noticeable change in the market [3]. Further digitization in the health sector will lead to more extensive exchange of sensitive patient data. Since the data requires special protection, the IT security has to be a major focus point.

This paper will describe some of the specific security considerations that need to be made in the healthcare branch when using IoT devices and cloud services. There are some specifics that need to be highlighted in this industry. In Section II, an overview of the status quo concerning IT security for medical applications is provided. Initial analysis of IoT devices and cloud services are presented in Sections III and IV, respectively. Both sections go into more detail specifically for the use cases homecare and integrated care. It shows the different special conditions of the environment from the IT security perspective. This can be used as a blueprint for dealing with cloud services and IoT devices in the healthcare sector.

II. Recent Work in Medical IT Security

With the current Covid-19 pandemic, it is obvious that the healthcare sector is forced to transform itself and adopt new telecommunication technologies more quickly. Therefore, medical IoT device manufacturers are eager to evolve their current hardware and develop additional cloud services, which can already be seen in the rapid digitization of the industrial sector. This trend raises several IT security challenges. Firstly, as mentioned with the development of medical IoT devices, manufacturers are trying to enlarge their business offerings by developing digital services. Secondly, it is obvious that due to financial restrictions medical healthcare facilities are going to integrate their out-of-date medical inventory into their existing IT infrastructure. It is obligatory to note that such devices were never designed to operate in an IoT network, therefore, lacking the required security design to operate in this environment. Additionally, for most older medical devices the original manufacturers either never intended to provide updates from the beginning or stopped doing so. The previously mentioned thoughts clearly illustrate upcoming vulnerabilities. As a consequence, several institutes and enclosed working groups are aiming to guide and regulate medical device manufacturers. An example for a guiding group is the Medical Device Coordination Group (MDCG) established by Article 103 of Regulation (EU) 2017/745. They published the "Guidance on Cybersecurity for medical devices" [4]. This Medical Device Directive represents a first basis of the ongoing research when it comes to implementing IT security in the field of network-connected medical devices. Also, the International Medical Device Regulators Forum (IMDRF) is investigating cyber threats and is aiming to "promote a globally harmonized approach to medical device cybersecurity that at a fundamental level ensures the safety and performance of medical devices and encouraging information" in their current work item "Medical Device Cybersecurity Guide" [5]. From a national perspective, the German Federal Office For Information Security (BSI) recently published the reports of their research projects "Manipulation in Medical Products" (ManiMed) and "Digitization in Care" (eCare). These documents contain recommendations for good IT security practices for medical manufacturers. The publication "Cyber Security Requirements for Network-Connected Medical Devices" [6] provides detailed assistance to manufacturers in how identified security threats can be reduced. Even if those concepts are developed, approved and implemented it is still vital to consider how they are embedded into their specific environment. In detail, it is important to differentiate the surroundings (e.g., private home, clinic, elderly home) into which medical IoT devices will be integrated, the technical capabilities of the targeted user and the individual IT landscape into which the devices are integrated.

III. Medical IoT

The Internet of Things is widely known as a landscape of interconnected devices that collect, send and store data over a network. After an initial setup, mostly no human-to-human or human-to-computer interaction is required. In contrast to classic devices, most IoT devices have features known as smart functions, which means that they can access information on the internet, as well as be accessed from outside their local network. In general, two types of IoT devices can be distinguished. While there are IoT devices that require another device (such as a smartphone) in order to establish a connection with the network indirectly, others are connected directly. In order to use IoT devices, connections between the devices are required. These connections can be wired, such as Ethernet, or wireless, e.g., USB, Bluetooth, 5G networks, WiFi and Zigbee, that should be considered in an IT security strategy. Especially in the field of healthcare, specific requirements for certain devices are needed, e.g., connectors for an ECG have standard requirements regarding safety (ANSI/AAMI EC53) [7]. A review of several guidelines and standard literature reveals that the recommendations and specifications are similar to each other and show almost no contradiction. In this respect, different sources of information are being used in this paper, which all have the same direction in approaching the desired security level. The productive usage of IoT devices has a variety of benefits. In relation to the health sector, IoT devices can proactively foresee health conditions and patients can be diagnosed, treated and monitored automatically. IoT devices increase the transparency in tracking of medical objects. Central management enables better visibility for a large number of devices at the same time. This offers an opportunity to relieve medical staff and let them focus on their actual work on patients. As a consequence, hospital stays can be reduced and re-admissions avoided [8]. However, these interconnections represent potential security weaknesses. In the following section potential threats concerning medical IoT devices are discussed. The focus is on general advice influenced by the top-level use cases homecare and integrated care, which are explained in detail in Section III-A and III-B, respectively.

First, a holistic security strategy must be created. This strategy needs to include the overarching infrastructure of the surrounding environment. It is crucial to distinguish whether the environment is safe and controllable (e.g., hospital network) or an unprotected area (e.g., in a patient's home). In any case, fine-grained access control mechanism and multi-level user administration have to be part of the deployment strategy. Otherwise, especially in unprotected surroundings, this could be an easy gateway for data theft or data manipulation [6]. An investigation by the BSI of six medical products (e.g., senior tablet, emergency watch with fall detection, etc.) shows that this has not been sufficiently taken into account so far. These devices were examined for security vulnerabilities. The bottom line remains: The IT security level of all devices is critical, as moderate to severe weaknesses were identified, which concludes that none of the devices were previously subjected to an IT security test. None of the devices met the requirements of ISO 27001 [9]. Since it is mostly sensitive patient data, encrypted data transmission is essential. The technical guideline TR-02102 of the BSI on cryptographic procedures should be included in the strategy [6].

If the configuration is adapted to the environment, it must be ensured that the specifications for secure implementation are adhered to before commissioning. In concrete terms, this means a separation of software units and the use of already certified and, therefore, approved implementations instead of in-house development of services or protocols. Before medical IoT devices are put into operation, it has to be ensured that the assignment of permissions is restricted by default. Only the privileges necessary for operation should be allowed at its lowest level.

After the devices have been configured and implemented, an automated, auditable and controllable update function must be offered in order to be able to close known vulnerabilities as quickly as possible. Patches and updates for medical IoT devices in Germany have to come from known and trustworthy sources [10].

A. Medical IoT in Homecare

The term homecare describes the treatment of patients with medical aids, dressings and medical diets at home or in nursing homes [11]. In the context of this research, the focus is solely on the applications at home. Products that are being used in nursing homes will be addressed in the Section "Integrated Care" below. In the homecare sector, various applications (e.g., wearables) can support the health system, such as remote monitoring of health progress, improving self-management of chronic conditions, early detection of anomalies, quick identification of symptoms or compliance with medication intake. However, the use of IoT equipment in a remote environment requires a well thought out strategy to allow reaping said benefits whilst neither compromising confidentiality nor integrity.

First, the characteristics of the environment in which an IoT device is to be deployed must be identified. This is necessary in order to derive the precautions, which are needed for secure operation. The home networks of patients differ vastly in size, complexity and given security. Devices of a home network are unknown and can change at any time. Additionally, it cannot be guaranteed that all network components within the network are state-of-the-art and that their software is being updated regularly. Therefore, the assumption of the worst case scenario has to be made and a generic home network has to be classified as a hostile environment. This requires thorough security hardening of the used IoT devices. A certain security level can be ensured by requiring relevant certifications from the manufacturer, but there are still no specific medical technical certifications, which completely fulfill the conditions of medical surroundings. Another option would be to request a penetration testing report from a well-known cyber security company, but for most applications this is not a suitable option. In practice this could lead to additional time and money, which needs to be spent by the customer if the IoT manufacturer cannot provide such a report by default. This can be justified if the product is used in critical applications. It is therefore highly dependent on the circumstances and the amount of risk that needs to be mitigated. The customers themselves can also proactively increase the network security independently of the manufacturer. A safeguard is network segmentation, where the goal is to completely separate the communication channels of the IoT device from the traffic of the remaining home network. The IoT device is then only able to communicate with its intended communication partners and it cannot be accessed from any other non-trusted network member.

Second, the consumer has to specify the expected benefits and features the product of the manufacturer is supposed to provide. The patients' IT skills have to be taken into consideration. Because a homecare provider has to provide their services to the entire demographic and all social classes, IT knowledge cannot be expected (e.g., elders). Therefore, the set up and maintenance needs to be done by an expert and it should not be possible for a patient to change any security parameters. The specifications also allow identification of communication interfaces which should be enabled or disabled. Reducing the amount of possible communication paths minimizes the attack surface. In the context of homecare this is even more important because of the unsecured and unprotected environment.

B. Medical IoT in Integrated Care

Integrated care is not a well defined term [12]. In this paper integrated care will be referred to as the aspiration to optimize workflows within medical facilities with the help of digitization and IoT. Such facilities could be hospitals, nursing homes, medical offices or any other institutions in the healthcare sector.

Deployment of an IoT device in an integrated care facility needs to be well thought out. The IT security of the IoT device itself must be guaranteed and a secure infrastructure must be available. As with the homecare use case, the first step is to determine how to integrate an IoT product into the network. It is an advantage that the infrastructure, into which a product is deployed, is completely under the customer's control. The customer might provide their patients with WiFi access, for example, so these connections can be seen as unknown members within the network. As a consequence, the patients' connection can be potential threats. But most of the time network segmentation is in place to strongly separate this kind of traffic from the internal communications of the facility. Thus, the focus will only be on integrating IoT devices into the closed off environment of the customer. From the perspective of the IoT device the network can be seen as a trusted environment. However, IoT devices themselves can only be trusted to a certain degree. According to Check Point Software Technologies Ltd. the risk of a data breach through IoT is substantial. It is advisable to the customer to deploy network segmentation in a way that the IoT device only has access to the endpoints, which are needed for it to operate [13].

Again, the specification of all needed features is the foundation that allows for the derivation of the customer's needed IT know-how, as well as the product's communication interfaces required. The customer needs to determine if it is within the capabilities of their staff to set up and maintain the IoT product in question. This depends on the amount of work force and knowledge available, as well as the complexity and number of the products. Additionally, it needs to be ensured that only system administrators are allowed to configure IT security parameters. The staff which is responsible for handling the device in operation then only requires the permission to configure and start the product on a medical level. This is particularly a problem in nursing homes, where there is often neither the required IT knowledge nor enough staff.

IV. Cloud Services

In Section III, the focus was on the security of the IoT device. In the following sections, the chain of communication from an IoT device to its respective cloud services is going to be analyzed. Hereby, a distinction between different types of cloud services is going to be made. At last, the specifics of integrated care as well as homecare are going to be discussed as well.

When it comes to deploying IoT in any environment, considering the device itself as part of the respective network is necessary, but any relationships to the cloud services it is connected to in order to provide either its intended functions or additional features are also relevant. Similarities can be drawn to the Industrial Internet of Things (IIoT). In the IIoT, connections to different services are needed in order provide firmware updates, receive sensor data, achieve remote maintenance, perform analytics and other services [14]. Each cloud service needs to fulfill specific tasks which can differ vastly in complexity and the amount of data which is sent or received over a certain period of time. Therefore, different interfaces, protocols and connection types are needed in order to ensure the desired functionality.

In the health sector an IoT device might be responsible for monitoring vital data of a patient (e.g., heart rate and blood pressure). The manufacturer might require a connection to their company servers in order to provide security and feature updates on the fly. A second connection might go to the infrastructure of the doctor or health personnel in charge in order to receive the measurements of the sensor for evaluation. Even more connections might be possible for remote maintenance and other services. The work in [15] goes into further detail on which applications might be possible and how such a cloud platform might be implemented. It can be seen that knowledge from industrial applications can be used as a foundation to build on for healthcare use cases. The main difference is that the handled information is far more sensitive and the requirements for availability and stability are far higher. In a worst case scenario a malfunction of the IoT device might decide over life and death.

Three entry points can be identified where a malicious actor might compromise security. The first being the connection itself from a client to the cloud service. In the following paragraph it is assumed that the way a connection is established and maintained from the client to the cloud is secure. This is justified because using common state of the art technology, such as Transport Layer Security (TLS) or a Virtual Private Networks (VPN), already ensures a high level of security. Furthermore, it is not the objective of this paper to evaluate common protocols or standards (e.g., Bluetooth). What is left is the possibility for an attacker to disrupt the connection, for example, with a Denial of Service (DOS) attack. An interruption of communication does not necessarily mean that a malicious actor is present. Other reasons might be technical difficulties of the provider or power outages. It is important for the customer to develop a process in which it is defined how an unexpected interruption is supposed to be handled. The maximum reaction time should be specified. The reaction time is defined as the time difference between the incident happening and the execution of the reaction. Both the steps necessary to handle a security incident and the maximum reaction time are highly dependent on the products and services used as well as the severity of a potential malfunction.

A second entry point might be the device itself. The ability to compromise an IoT device has security implications on the cloud services. Taking control of a device, which is connected to a cloud service, must not lead to a security breach of the cloud service. This can be achieved by minimizing the permissions an IoT device has within the corresponding cloud infrastructure. The provider of the cloud service is responsible for these security measures. Taking a look at the example of monitoring vital data mentioned above the device should only be able to receive updates and send sensor data. When receiving updates the only thing being sent by the device should be the credentials to gain access to said updates. When sending sensor data, only valid data sets are supposed to be accepted by the cloud service. Should the cloud service accept any malformed data sets or instructions, then security might be at risk. Malicious instructions might be sent which were not intended to be executed by design. Then the doors are potentially open for privilege escalation attacks and much more.

The last entry point is the cloud service itself for the IoT devices. This is the most crucial component. A breach of security in the cloud service not only puts at risk the availability or confidentiality of a single device but of all devices using that service. Additionally, other cloud services, which are connected to the compromised instance, in order to further process data, might be affected, too. Depending on the use case the cloud service may require extensive hardening. Guidelines and certifications help ensure the desired level of security. Again, the number of measures that need to be taken depends on the intended use cases and the requirements on the different security goals.

A. *Cloud Services in Homecare*

As previously established in Section III-A a home network is an inherently hostile environment, therefore, any connection to it must be verified as thoroughly as possible. As a result, each type of application that is supposed to be used in a homecare scenario has to be set up with certain precautions in order to provide a high level of security.

Three major homecare application types have been identified. First, there are management applications for staff in the field. These services help nurses, doctors and other personnel to manage and document every day tasks, patients' health records, schedule appointments and meetings as well as allow them to use the available work force as efficiently as possible. The second category is cloud applications that provide status updates to the patients. Here patients get access to all information related to their treatment. Additional features might be the ability to request appointments or ask questions related to the treatment directly online. The last and most important category for this paper are cloud services, which are connected to the medical IoT devices in the field. These services are responsible for receiving the data that is being collected as well as managing the devices by providing updates or doing remote management tasks.

Management platforms for the nursing staff are very potent tools when it comes to improving the quality of service. Because a staff member has access to the data of various patients the attack surface needs to be as small as possible. This can be done by only allowing managed work devices. These are then able to establish a secure connection to the respective cloud service. A secure connection might be realized with a VPN tunnel. VPNs require competent IT staff in order to operate securely. This has to be kept in mind when considering VPNs as an option because if the required work force and know-how is not present, such a solution will not be implemented properly, leaving the connections vulnerable again.

Patients can be given online access to updates of their treatments or the possibility to request appointments. In most cases these services will be provided over a web interface. Securing it can be a complex task because in the end it is a website with access to patient data. It is important that the provider follows good practices in web development in order to prevent vulnerabilities such as the Open Web Application Security

Project's (OWASP) "Top 10 Web Application Security Risks" [16]. Additionally, the amount of information provided to the patient should be restricted to only what is of relevance to them to limit the amount of information leaked in case of a security breach.

When it comes to monitoring IoT devices, which might send vital parameters to the nursing staff over a cloud service, either in intervals or continuously, it is essential that the connection to their respective platform is sufficiently encrypted and that only authorized devices are allowed to send (and receive) data. VPN tunnels might be an option, which allows the connection from the medical applications to be separated from all potentially malicious network traffic in a patient's home. However, even then the risk remains that an attack consumes the complete bandwidth of the internet connection resulting in a violation of availability.

Before integrating any of the three application types into their productive IT infrastructure, the customer of the cloud service needs to find out how the provider aims to prevent attacks on their products. This is essential because then the customer can compare the measures which have already been taken to their own requirements and evaluate if the level of security is sufficient for their needs.

B. Cloud Services in Integrated Care

In Integrated Care, the network that is supported by a cloud service is completely owned and controlled by the customer. Integrating a cloud service into one's infrastructure can be done in a way that both systems are more interlinked than they would be otherwise. This allows for more possibilities to optimize the workflows within the corresponding premises. Due to the vast amount of possible applications in this context, it is not feasible for this research to cover all possibilities in a competent manner. Instead the focus is on the cloud as an intermediary between IoT devices and the infrastructure of a customer. Data is being sent by the IoT devices to the cloud, where it is being stored to enable the staff of the customer to retrieve the needed information.

In order to assess the necessary precautions that need to be taken, two parameters are to be determined. First, finding out how sensitive/valuable the data sets or assets are, which need to be protected, is necessary. Second, it is important to evaluate the amount of trust that can be given to a potential cloud service provider. Both factors dictate to what extent patient data needs to be protected. For example, if the collected data contains location information of a patient and the service provider is also known to offer commercial activity tracking and other analytics services to customers it can be expected that the service provider is interested in the data sets as well for their own commercial profit [17]. It is then necessary to encrypt the information given to the cloud service provider in order to prevent sensitive information to be leaked to unwanted third parties. An approach where this has been put into practice can be seen in [18] and [19].

Optimally, a zero trust policy is to be established, where access to patient data is only granted to staff who need insight into the data for operation. Due to resource limitations this can not always be put into practice. It is vital for the customer to build a legal framework, where the cloud service provider can be held responsible for neglecting the security of patient data. This should be done in two ways. First, it has to be ensured that the cloud service provider is a trusted and certified entity, where the required know-how exists to provide comprehensive security and service. Certifications such as ISO 27001 are good indicators as to whether the potential service provider takes their information security seriously. Additionally, the customer should not only define the measures that need to be taken by the provider to protect the data from leaks to third parties in a written agreement, but should also record what the cloud service provider is allowed or restricted to do with the stored data. This should be done to avoid any unwanted analytics done by the cloud service provider, which could potentially leak sensitive patient data unwillingly. Finally, security and privacy audits should be carried out on a regular basis.

V. 5G4HEALTHCARE

The mentioned use cases homcare and integrated care are also the main focus of the research project 5G4Healthcare funded by the German Federal Ministry of Transport and Digital Infrastructure. Its goal is to explore the effectiveness and efficiency of healthcare services to derive recommendations for scalable solutions with the help of 5G technology. IT security is a crucial workstream within the project. So far, medical technologies (e.g., mobile ultrasound devices, televisit trolleys, medical robots) have been purchased within the project and are being examined with regard to IT security. The results of the investigations are still pending. However, due to the sensitive data, the relevance of IT security is high, since simply changing medium of communication does not guarantee higher security, which could be a misconception due to the novelty of the 5G technology.

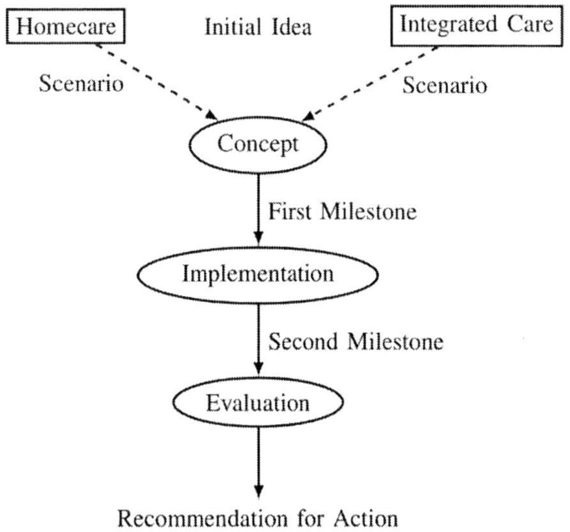

Figure 1. Workflow of a test scenario used by the 5G4Healthcare research project.

As can be seen in Figure 1, application scenarios are designed for the two use cases integrated care and homecare (phase 1), implemented in model form (phase 2) and tested and evaluated (phase 3). A platform based on 5G will be established, that enables testing and evaluation of digital applications in living labs (real-world environments) and test beds. So far it turned out that 5G applications in healthcare must meet essential requirements such as reliability, availability and confidentiality for rapid and high-volume data transmission. 5G enables the continuously increasing capacities of digital applications in terms of bandwidth, availability and latency, which are prioritized differently depending on the application. Most of the products used in the test scenarios are IoT devices with their associated cloud services. These scenarios demand for extensive security evaluation in parallel to the main objective of the research project. Details of the research results will be published in future.

VI. Conclusion and Outlook

This paper points out the need for common IT security guidelines and independent testing laboratories when designing and using medical IoT devices in productive environments. Institutes, regulators and others are currently focusing on developing recommendations and guidelines for IoT manufacturers but no proper entity checks on a regular basis or even worse, never, if manufactures comply with approved guidelines. Moreover, current guidelines do not take into account different environments, e.g., public hospitals or private homes, where medical IoT devices are going to be used. The authors conclude from the analysis made above, that different environments require different set-ups and different configurations. As a result different levels of certain IT-skills are needed for secure operation when embedding medical IoT devices in an existing IT infrastructure. Also, it is obvious that manufacturers are aiming to enlarge their IoT product portfolio by developing supporting cloud services and platforms. The additional cloud service offerings underpin the fact that in contrast to the fourth industrial revolution IoT devices, medical IoT devices need to comply to stricter requirements and should be required to pass recurring testing cycles by specific medical independent regulators. Doing so benefits the patient's well-being and trust. Otherwise, a wide adaptation of trustworthy medical IoT devices in the sensitive healthcare sector is doomed to fail. Mastering those upcoming challenges, which are going to exponentially grow by adopting 5G, must be unequivocally investigated from different perspectives such as environment, users and certifications to guarantee a trustworthy development and usage life cycle. First and foremost, it is obvious that a fine-grained segmentation of IoT devices based on their levels of sensitivity in usage is vital to support the administration and monitoring of sensitive IoT devices and finally ensure a secure operating environment.

VII. Acknowledgement

This research is funded as part of recently granted 5G4Healthcare project by the German Federal Ministry of Transport and Digital Infrastructure within the 5x5G Initiative.

References

[1] Check Point Software Technologies Ltd., "Cyber Security Report 2020," 2020. [Online]. Available: https://www.ntsc.org/assets/pdfs/cyber-security-report-2020.pdf [retrieved: 2021.03.02]

[2] Transforma Insights, "IoT Connected Devices Worldwide 2019-2030," *Statista*, 2020. [Online]. Available: https://www.statista.com/statistics/1183457/iot-connected-devices-worldwide/ [retrieved: 2021.03.02]

[3] T. Thranberend and T. Kostera, "Digitale Gesundheit: Deutschland hinkt hinterher [Digital Health: Germany is lagging behind]," 2018. [Online]. Available: https://www.bertelsmann-stiftung.de/de/themen/aktuelle-meldungen/2018/november/digitale-gesundheit-deutschland-hinkt-hinterher [retrieved: 2021.03.02]

[4] Medical Device Coordination Group, "MDCG 2019-16 Guidance on Cyber Security for Medical Devices," Dec. 2019. [Online]. Available: https://ec.europa.eu/docsroom/documents/41863/attachments/1/translations/en/renditions/native [retrieved: 2021.03.02]

[5] International Medical Device Regulators Forum, "Medical Device Cybersecurity Guide," 2021. [Online]. Available: http://www.imdrf.org/workitems/wi-mdc-guide.asp [retrieved: 2021.03.02]

[6] Bundesamt für Sicherheit in der Informationstechnik, "Cyber Security Requirements for Network-Connected Medical Devices," Nov. 2018. [Online]. Available: https://www.bsi.bund.de/SharedDocs/Downloads/EN/BSI/ICS/Medical_Devices_CS-E_132.pdf [retrieved: 2021.03.02]

[7] D. Guttadauro, "Electrical Connectors: Design Considerations for Medical Devices," 2019. [Online]. Available: https://www.medicaldesignbriefs.com/component/content/article/mdb/features/articles/33986 [retrieved: 2021.03.02]

[8] GMO GlobalSign Ltd., "Das Gesundheitswesen der Zukunft: Das IoT prägt die Branche schon jetzt [Healthcare of the Future: IoT is already shaping the industry]," Sep. 2018. [Online]. Available: https://www.globalsign.com/de-de/blog/iot-gesundheitswesen-der-zukunft [retrieved: 2021.03.02]

[9] Bundesamt für Sicherheit in der Informationstechnik, "eCare - Digitalisierung in der Pflege - eine aktuelle Marktanalyse und IT-Sicherheitsbetrachtung [eCare - Digitization in Nursing Care - A current market analysis and IT security review]," Dec. 2020. [Online]. Available: https://www.bsi.bund.de/SharedDocs/Downloads/DE/BSI/ DigitaleGesellschaft/eCare_Abschlussbericht.pdf [retrieved: 2021.03.02]

[10] Bundesamt für Sicherheit in der Informationstechnik, "SYS.4.4 Allgemeines IoT-Gerät [SYS.4.4 General IoT Device]," 2021. [Online]. Available: https://www.bsi.bund.de/SharedDocs/Downloads/DE/BSI/Grundschutz/Kompendium_Einzel_PDFs/07_SYS_IT_Systeme/SYS_4_4_Allgemeines_IoT_Geraet_Edition_2020.pdf [retrieved: 2021.03.02]

[11] Bundesverband Medizintechnologie, "Homecare," 2021. [Online]. Available: https://www.bvmed.de/de/versorgung/homecare [retrieved: 2021.03.02]

[12] D. L. Kodner and C. Spreeuwenberg, "Integrated Care: Meaning, Logic, Applications, and Implications – a Discussion Paper," *International Journal of Integrated Care*, vol. 2, no. 4, Nov. 2002. [Online]. Available: http://www.ijic.org/article/10.5334/ijic.67/ [retrieved: 2021.03.29]

[13] Check Point Software Technologies Ltd., "Healthcare Breaches Affected Nearly One Million US Patients: The Security Risks of Medical IoT," May 2019. [Online]. Available: https://blog.checkpoint.com/2019/05/29/ultrasound-iot-hack-security-risks-healthcare-medical-device-michigan-ransomware/ [retrieved: 2021.03.02]

[14] M. Molle *et al.*, "Security of Cloud Services with Low-Performance Devices in Critical Infrastructures," in *The Tenth International Conference on Cloud Computing, GRIDs, and Virtualization*, B. Duncan, Y. W. Lee, M. Westerlund, and A. Aßmuth, Eds., International Academy, Research, and Industry Association. International Academy, Research, and Industry Association, 2019, pp. 88–89.

[15] S. Bharati, P. Podder, M. R. H. Mondal, and P. K. Paul, *Applications and Challenges of Cloud Integrated IoMT*. Cham: Springer International Publishing, 2021, pp. 67–85.

[16] Open Web Application Security Project, "OWASP top ten web application security risks," 2017. [Online]. Available: https://owasp.org/www-project-top-ten/ [retrieved: 2021.03.02]

[17] S. Sharma, K. Chen, and A. Sheth, "Toward Practical Privacy-Preserving Analytics for IoT and Cloud-Based Healthcare Systems," *IEEE Internet Computing*, vol. 22, no. 2, pp. 42–51, 2018.

[18] M. Anuradha *et al.*, "IoT enabled cancer prediction system to enhance the authentication and security using cloud computing," *Microprocessors and Microsystems*, vol. 80, p. 103301, 2021.

[19] R. Denis and P. Madhubala, "Hybrid data encryption model integrating multi-objective adaptive genetic algorithm for secure medical data communication over cloud-based healthcare systems," *Multimedia Tools and Applications*, mar 2021.

A Secure and Privacy-Friendly Logging Scheme

Andreas Aßmuth[1], Robert Duncan[3], Simon Liebl[1,2], and Matthias Söllner[1]

[1]Technical University of Applied Sciences OTH Amberg-Weiden
Amberg, Germany
Email: {a.assmuth | s.liebl | m.soellner}@oth-aw.de
[2]PhD Student at Abertay University, Dundee, UK
[3]University of Aberdeen
Aberdeen, United Kingdom
Email: robert.duncan@abdn.ac.uk

***Abstract*—Finding a robust security mechanism for audit trail logging has long been a poorly satisfied goal. There are many reasons for this. The most significant of these is that the audit trail is a highly sought after goal of attackers to ensure that they do not get caught. Thus they have an incredibly strong incentive to prevent companies from succeeding in this worthy aim. Regulation, such as the European Union General Data Protection Regulation, has brought a strong incentive for companies to achieve success in this area due to the punitive level of fines that can now be levied in the event of a successful breach by an attacker. We seek to resolve this issue through the use of an encrypted audit trail process that saves encrypted records to a true immutable database, which can ensure audit trail records are permanently retained in encrypted form, with no possibility of the records being compromised. This ensures compliance with the General Data Protection Regulation can be achieved.**

***Index Terms*—logging; audit trail; cryptography; privacy; security.**

I. Introduction

Today, we all are used to authenticate ourselves in order to access systems and services we use in our everyday life. Authentication can be viewed from two different perspectives. For ourselves and especially for our private use, authentication ensures that no one else can access our data. For the system or service provider, authentication is used to distinguish between users. Different users may have different subscriptions for the services and, for example, the service provider is not interested in users using services for free that should be paid for. Additionally, the system provider might get contacted by authorities or law enforcement agencies if illegal actions have occurred involving their services. In this case, authentication is used to determine which user is responsible for the illegal actions and which users were not involved at all.

At work, it is common practice that several employees share a computer or work with one industrial machine. And of course, Cloud-based services and applications allow multiple employees to work on a project collaboratively. In all these systems, it is important to identify and authenticate the current user in order to grant him or her the appropriate privileges. In order to trace who, for example, has processed an order, the digital identity of the employee is saved and logged. In the event of a severe mistake, a negligent operation on an expensive machine or illegal actions, the company wants to ensure to be able to track down the responsible employee. And if we additionally take compliance to security and privacy regulations into account, we must consider so called malicious insider actions as well. These are incidents that were deliberately caused by (former) employees who want to stain the companies reputation or damage the company's equipment. According to a study by the Ponemon Institute, more than 70 % of participating companies have had more than ten insider-related incidents within a year [1].

Features and services that are used to track individual actions to single employees can be viewed critically because such measures can violate the privacy of employees. One such example is the so called "productivity score" [2], which has raised much criticism and was condemned by the press as a means for workplace surveillance [3] [4]. But even without such services, permanent monitoring employees may be used to assess their productivity. Therefore, especially companies with a strong workers' council are looking for other solutions. Finding such solutions is often also in the company's executive's interest because some companies have been fined in recent years for violations of the General Data Protection Regulation (GDPR). For example, in 2020, the Hamburg Commissioner for Data Protection and Freedom of Information fined H & M (Hennes & Mauritz) € 35.3 million for data protection violations of employees' personal data. The company recorded a considerable amount of highly personal data about their employees' vacation experiences, but also symptoms of illness and diagnoses. In addition, some supervisors acquired a broad knowledge of their employees' private lives through personal and floor talks, ranging from rather harmless details to family issues and religious beliefs. Some of this knowledge was recorded, digitally stored and partly readable by up to 50 other managers throughout the company. The recordings were sometimes made with a high level of detail and recorded over greater periods of time documenting the development of these issues. This practice only came to light when the data became accessible company wide following a misconfiguration error, following which the regulator became involved [5].

Finding a solution to this problem, to be capable of tracking down individuals without violating their privacy, is not trivial. Going back to shady practices some companies used before they discovered the necessity of being able to track down an employees actions if needed, is definitely no suitable solution. Imagine a manufacturing company assigns a group of employees to machine. This would allow to assess the whole team, but would not violate the privacy of individual employees. But in case of mistakes, illegal actions, etc., the company then would not be capable of tracking down the responsible employee. In practice, this approach leads to additional drawbacks concerning security. In order to facilitate work, in this approach such groups of employees very often use only a single, usually rather weak password that is easy to remember (or may even be found on a sticker right at the machine) instead of having strong individual passwords. In case of sabotage by an employee, the responsible person cannot be determined because he or she does not even have to belong to that group of employees.

This paper is structured as follows: in Section II, we describe possible logging strategies before we address security and privacy challenges in Section III. In Section IV, we present our solution for a secure and privacy-friendly logging scheme and further ideas, how our solution can be modified in order to fulfil special or additional requirements. We conclude in Section V with an outlook on future work.

II. Logging Strategies

Logging is usually carried out for the purpose of providing an audit trail of all activities involved in running the system. This is a practice that has long been carried out in the accounting profession to ensure a robust mechanism exists such that in the event of a disaster, the audit trail may be used to restore the accounting records in order to reconstitute the accounts of the organisation. Of course, once logging for this purpose started to be carried out in electronic systems, smart attackers realised that due to inherent weaknesses in database systems, by attacking the audit trail, it was possible to remove evidence of their incursion into the system by deleting or modifying the audit trail records.

While a number of early database systems offered an immutable database option, there were a number of challenges that needed to be overcome. First, the immutable database could not use key fields, meaning retrieval or analysis of the contents of the database would be both cumbersome and slow. Second, and perhaps more importantly, there was nothing to prevent the entire database from being deleted once the attacker gained entry and has escalated sufficient privileges.

This meant that the use of traditional database systems would not be sufficient to achieve our requirements to retain a secure audit trail through logging. This brought about the need to find an alternative immutable database solution instead. One option would have been to use blockchain, which provides the core security for crypto-currencies. However, there is a potential significant overhead in going down this route. The public blockchain relies on thousands of nodes, which are required to perform extensive cryptographic algorithmic computations to ensure a proper consensus of the contents of the blockchain can be guaranteed, but this brings a huge overhead to the equation, since those who perform the cryptographic tasks are looking for a reward for the considerable efforts they provide, meaning considerable extra costs of operation, along with a lesser level of performance due to the huge redundancy on offer.

The alternative solution here would be for the corporate to use a private blockchain, but this also brings challenges. This private blockchain would be provisioned by the corporate, but now their challenge would be to find a balance between choosing the minimal level of blockchain redundancy to improve latency, against being able to retain a sufficient number of nodes securely enough to retain full control over the contents of the blockchain.

However, in 2020, a new start company introduced immudb [6], a lightweight, high-speed immutable database that is specifically designed to complement existing transactional database systems. It is tailor made to track changes in the main database system and to then record these transactions, or logs, in the tamperproof immudb. The immudb system gives you the same cryptographic verification of the integrity of data written with SHA-256 like classic blockchain without the cost and complexity associated with blockchains today. This means that unlike traditional transaction logs, which are very hard to scale, immudb is extremely fast, scalable, robust and open source, making it ideal to incorporate for this purpose. For further details on the immutable storage we refer to [7].

III. Security and Privacy Challenges

Security and privacy challenges in this area are not new. In 1999, Schneier and Kelsey [8] set out to secure the collection of sensitive logs using encryption, to ensure that forensic records could be maintained in the event of a cyber breach. Some five years later, Waters et al. [9], realised that system logs were becoming a prime attack vector for attackers, who were seeking to cover their trail after successfully breaking in to computer systems. The authors felt that improved searchability would be an asset in dealing with a subsequent forensic examination, and they sought to provide a rapid search function to interrogate this encrypted data. Further, they implemented an audit log for database queries using hash chains for integrity protection and identity-based encryption with extracted keywords to enable better searching. Over a decade later, Syta et al. [10], felt that such was the interest of attackers in this area that further strengthening of systems would be necessary to ensure proper protection could be achieved. The authors attempted to allow a considerable increase in scale, as well as the development of multi-signatures to provide further protection. Their system is claimed to protect against man-in-the-middle attacks.

IV. Example Logging Approach

The logging scheme we propose consists of two basic components: (a) an appropriate secret sharing scheme and (b) an immutable storage. Readers who are already familiar with immutable storage and secret sharing schemes may want to skip the according subsections.

A. Immutable Storage

The reason we seek to use immutable storage is to ensure that we can only ever add new records to the database. We are not ever allowed to modify or delete records. This will allow us to create entries of permanent record with which to store any information related to the authentication of employees. This will prevent any party from interfering with any entry of permanent record, ensuring we are able to retain permanency of all such transactions. This will provide an audit trail of all transactions relating to employees. Regardless of whether any attack comes from an external source, or from a malicious inside party, they will not be able to alter any of these records. The data that is stored in this immutable storage is encrypted in order to fulfil the demanded privacy constraints. Since is not possible to tamper with the data stored in this immutable storage, even gaining access to the data will not reveal any interesting details to the attacker.

B. Secret Sharing

The idea of secret sharing is as follows: some data D is divided into n pieces, $D_1, \ldots, D_n$, in such a way that D can be reconstructed of any $k < n$ pieces D_i. Additionally, it is ensured that the knowledge of $k-1$ or less pieces D_i is not sufficient to reconstruct D. In this case, the reconstruction ends up with a completely undetermined set of bits. Adi Shamir proposed a secret sharing scheme in 1979 that is based upon polynomial interpolation [11]. To emphasise the importance of the two integers n and k, Shamir named such a secret sharing scheme a "(k, n) threshold scheme". Following Shamir's blueprint, D is associated with an integer smaller than some prime number $p > D$. For k points $(x_i, y_i) \in \mathrm{GF}(p) \times \mathrm{GF}(p)$, $i = 1, \ldots, k$, with distinct coordinates x_i, there exists one and only one polynomial q of degree $k-1$, such that $q(x_i) = y_i$ holds for all $i = 1, \ldots, k$. For the polynomial

$$q(x) = \sum_{i=0}^{k-1} a_i x^i$$

the coefficients a_1 to a_{k-1} are chosen randomly and the coefficient a_0 is used to store D, so $a_0 = D$. In order to obtain the n different pieces $D_1, \ldots, D_n$, the function values of the indices are computed:

$$D_i = q(i), \quad i = 1, \ldots, n.$$

From any subset of k elements D_i, the coefficients a_i can be computed, provided that their identifying indices are known. After the polynomial q has been revealed, the reconstruction of the data D is achieved by computing $q(0) = a_0 = D$. If Shamir's secret sharing scheme is intended to be used, the first step is to specify k, the number of pieces needed for the reconstruction of D. The total number of pieces then is $n = 2k - 1$. As pointed out before,

$$k = \left\lceil \frac{n+1}{2} \right\rceil$$

or more pieces D_i allow the reconstruction of D, whereas less than k,

$$k - 1 = \left\lfloor \frac{n}{2} \right\rfloor$$

are not sufficient.

Blakley's solution to the secret sharing problem is based on finite geometry [12]. He suggested to encode the secret as a coordinate of a point in a k-dimensional space. The basic idea of Blakley's secret sharing scheme is that any k nonparallel $(k-1)$-dimensional hyperplanes intersect at a specific point which in this case contains the secret. In order to generate the secret shares, n hyperplane equations are computed using the intersection coordinates and additional random numbers modulo a prime number p. Any k or more out of these n hyperplane equations may be used to construct a system of linear equations that can easily be solved in order to obtain the secret provided that the determinant of the coefficient matrix formed of the given hyperplane equations is nonzero modulo p.

For these two traditional secret sharing schemes, the shares are at least of the same size as the secret itself. The authors of this paper have successfully used secret sharing schemes before, e.g., in order to store log files of the nodes of a Cloud system in a decentralised way [13]–[15]. For applications like this, that require secret sharing schemes to be applied to large amounts of data, this is probably unfavourable. In this case, the work of Krawczyk should be helpful who found out that if the notion of secrecy is reduced to computational instead of information theoretic secrecy, a remarkable amount of space and communication can be reduced [16]. But as the next subsection is going to clarify, this is not a problem for the proposed logging scheme, because the secret sharing scheme is used to secure only a small amount of data, namely the private key of a public key encryption scheme.

C. Proposed Logging Scheme

On the basis of the two core components, immutable storage and secret sharing, we describe our solution to the problem in this subsection. Our solution can be applied to a single company site, but also to multiple sites of a (larger) company, which are located in different countries and interconnected using a Cloud service.

To achieve maximum security, all persons must authenticate themselves using individual accounts on the system. Preferably, two-factor authentication should be used. The information, who logged into the system at which time, must be stored encrypted in order to prevent unauthorised personnel from reading this sensitive information. Since we have a system for a whole company in mind, it seems plausible to assume there are several computers or machines that all need to be in the logging system because employees log into all of these computers and machines. All of these devices must be capable of encrypting their logging information and, therefore, need an encryption key to be stored on each device. For our logging system, we choose a public-key encryption scheme, so the encryption key may be stored on all of these devices and is assumed to be publicly known. An encryption scheme with symmetric keys that uses the same key for encryption and decryption is not suitable in this case because of the necessity to have the encryption key stored on a large number of devices. This secret key might fall into the hands of an unauthorised person, e.g., from a single unsecured computer, and this person would then also be capable of reading all the sensitive logging information. Thus, in order to be able to read the sensitive information, the corresponding private key is required for decryption. This key is not stored on these computers and machines because there is no need to decrypt the data locally. The private key is divided into a number of parts, e.g., into three parts: one part for the employer, one part for the workers' council representing the employees and one part for law enforcement authorities. It might be sensible to have more or other groups, therefore, we do not stick to this example but just count these different groups, which all get a part of the secret key. It must be stressed that all of these parts are needed to reconstruct the private key in order to decrypt the encrypted logging data. So all of the groups must agree and combine their private key parts (AND operation). Figure 1 depicts the fragmentation of the private key and the

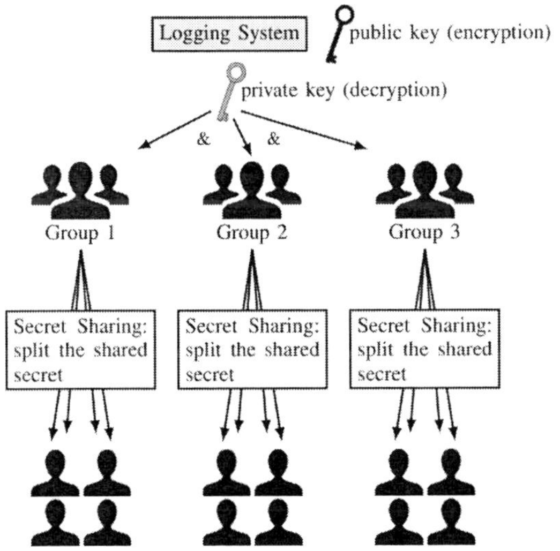

Figure 1. Distribution of the private key among several groups and persons.

distribution of the parts to three groups. In practice, these parts of the private key would possibly be in possession of one person of the respective group. But this would be quite unfavourable because this makes that single person a high-value target for attacks that aim to get the respective part of the secret key. Additionally, if there is an incident, it must be dealt with instantly. It would be unacceptable if that one person would then be in another shift, ill at home or on leave. That one person might also be threatened or bribed to give access to his or her part of the secret key; or that person might accidentally loose or delete their part of the private key. For all these reasons, it makes sense to divide the secret key part of each group into pieces using a secret sharing scheme. These pieces are then given to n persons of each group and it takes k of them to agree in order to merge the private key part of the group.

To sum up, this logging system supports both: security and privacy. Employees use their strong individual credentials for authentication. But they must not fear workplace surveillance or an unauthorised assessment of their productivity because their employer is not capable of reading the log files arbitrarily. In case an incident occurs and there is an official investigation, the different groups combine their parts to reconstruct the private key for the decryption of the log files. For each group, access to the respective part of the secret key is granted if a majority of group members (k out of n) agree.

D. Adaptability to Certain Scenarios

The presented scheme proposes that the different groups have to combine their parts of the private key to get the full private key and gain access. As the parts of the private key are combined with an AND operation, all groups have to contribute to gain access. On the other side scenarios might be interesting and desirable, where it would be sufficient when only j out of m groups come together to combine their keys in order to access the data. For this purpose the logging scheme can be adapted to share the private key among the groups also with the same secret sharing principle and inside a group the shared part can be shared with this scheme as proposed above (cf. Figure 2).

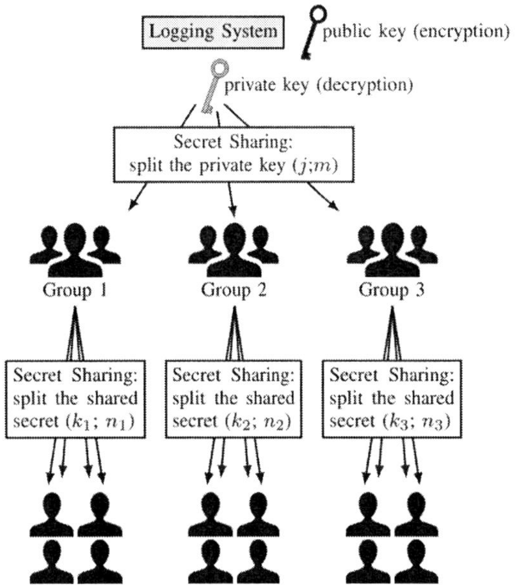

Figure 2. Adaption of the system: Secret Sharing among groups.

By using this adapted scheme it is possible to gain access to the secret, if only j out of m groups come together to combine the private key and in every group it would take only k out of n members of this group to agree to reconstruct their part of the shared secret. As it is only a matter of design, how many group members are needed to reconstruct their partial secret, the scheme can be adapted very flexibly to different scenarios: Each group g can have its own k_g and n_g. So, for example, group 1 has size n_1 and k_1 members of this group have to agree, group 2 may be much larger ($n_2 > n_1$) but fewer members (k_2) are needed in order to reconstruct their group's part of the secret key, and so on.

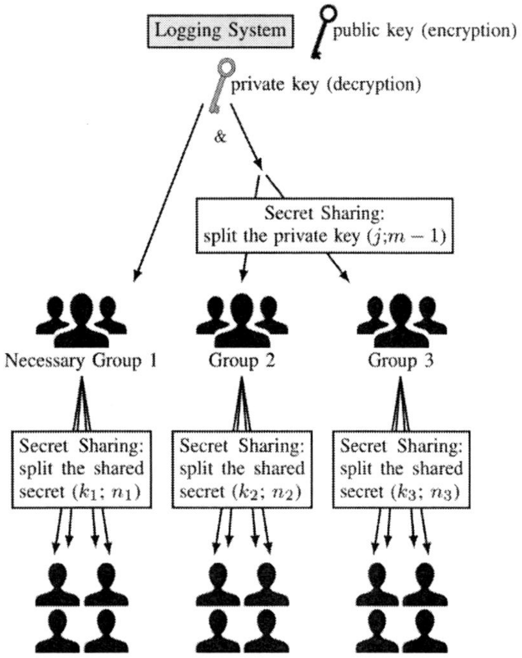

Figure 3. Further adaption of the system: Secret Sharing among groups and making one group necessary.

Furthermore, it is also possible to include one or more groups, which have to contribute necessarily (e.g., group 1 in Figure 3), because it is possible to combine AND operation and secret sharing on the group level, too. This means the private key is first split in two (or more to include more necessary groups) parts, which have to be combined again with AND operation later. One of this parts can then be distributed with secret sharing, the other parts are only shared within the necessary groups.

V. Conclusion and Future Work

As a first step, we have developed a highly secure logging approach for logging events connected with employees within the organisation. The logging data is captured and fully encrypted to ensure full compliance with the GDPR for any PII relating to employees of the organisation, since the data cannot be identified by anyone other than the duly authorised users of the system. We have demonstrated that this approach can deliver exactly the high security level of employee privacy which we were seeking.

Our next step will be to plan for the implementation of a proof-of-concept solution. As part of this process, we would test the outcome and performance of the system using differing secret sharing schemes to ensure we can deliver the most effective and powerful solution. However, we would also consider the possibility of investigating the development of how a verifiable secret sharing solution might further improve our suggested scheme.

Once we have reached that stage, we would seek to carry out an investigation into possible practical issues and endeavour to recognise any remaining problems with this work. We consider there may be the possibility of a collaboration between the two universities, OTH Amberg-Weiden and the University of Aberdeen.

References

[1] Ponemon Institute, Ed., "2018 Cost of Insider Threats: Global", April 2018, [Online]. Available: https://153j3ttjub71nfe89mc7r5gb-wpengine.netdna-ssl.com/wp-content/uploads/2018/04/ObserveIT-Insider-Threat-Global-Report-FINAL.pdf [accessed: 2021-04-01]

[2] Microsoft, Ed., "Microsoft Productivity Score", [Online]. Available: https://adoption.microsoft.com/productivity-score/ [accessed: 2021-04-01]

[3] A. Hern, "Microsoft productivity score feature criticised as workplace surveillance", The Guardian, [Online]. Available: https://www.theguardian.com/technology/2020/nov/26/microsoft-productivity-score-feature-criticised-workplace-surveillance, 2020-11-26 [accessed: 2021-04-01]

[4] S. Hurtz, "Angestellte überwachen? Microsoft macht's möglich", Süddeutsche Zeitung, [Online]. Available: https://sz.de/1.5130228, 2020-11-27 [accessed: 2021-04-01]

[5] Hamburg Commissioner, Ed., "35.3 Million Euro Fine for Data Protection Violations in H&M's Service Center", Datenschutz-Hamburg GDPR fine for GDPR employee data breach, Press Release, 2020. [Online]. Available: https://datenschutz-hamburg.de/assets/pdf/2020-10-01-press-release-h+m-fine.pdf [accessed: 2021-04-01]

[6] D. Zimmer, "immudb", 2021, [Online]. Available: https://www.codenotary.com/technologies/immudb/ [accessed: 2021-03-03]

[7] M. Paik, J. Irazábal, D. Zimmer, M. Meloni, and V. Padurean, "immudb: A Lightweight, Performant Immutable Database", Available: https://www.codenotary.com/technologies/immudb/ [accessed: 2021-04-01]

[8] B. Schneier and J. Kelsey, "Secure audit logs to support computer forensics", ACM Transactions on Information and System Security (TISSEC), 2(2), pp. 159-176, 1999.

[9] B. R. Waters, D. Balfanz, G. Durfee, and D. K. Smetters, "Building an Encrypted and Searchable Audit Log", NDSS, 4, pp. 5-6, 2004.

[10] E. Syta et al., "Keeping authorities 'honest or bust' with decentralized witness cosigning", 2016 IEEE Symposium on Security and Privacy (SP), pp. 526-545, 2016.

[11] A. Shamir, "How to share a secret", Communications of the ACM, vol. 22, no. 11, pp. 612-613, 1979.

[12] G. R. Blakley, "Safeguarding cryptographic keys", Managing Requirements Knowledge, International Workshop on (AFIPS), Proceedings, pp. 313-317, 1979.

[13] G. Weir and A. Aßmuth, "Strategies for Intrusion Monitoring in Cloud Services", pp. 49-53, 2017.

[14] G. Weir, A. Aßmuth, and N. Jäger, "Forensic Recovery and Intrusion Monitoring in the Cloud", International Journal on Advances in Security, vol. 11, no. 3 & 4, pp. 264-263, 2018.

[15] G. Weir, A. Aßmuth, M. Whittington, and B. Duncan, "Cloud Accounting Systems, the Audit Trail, Forensics and the EU GDPR: How Hard Can It Be?" BAFA Scottish Area Group Annual Conference 2017, Aberdeen, 2017.

[16] H. Krawczyk, "Secret Sharing Made Short", Advances in Cryptology CRYPTO' 93, Proceedings, Lecture Notes in Computer Science, vol. 773, pp. 136-146, Springer, 1993.

An Approach for Decentralized Authentication in Networks of UAVs

Nicholas Jäger and Andreas Aßmuth
Technical University of Applied Sciences OTH Amberg-Weiden
Department of Electrical Engineering, Media and Computer Science
Kaiser-Wilhelm-Ring 23, 92224 Amberg, Germany
email: {n.jaeger|a.assmuth}@oth-aw.de

Abstract—**We propose a decentralized authentication system for networks of unmanned aerial vehicles. A blockchain-based public key infrastructure allows the usage of public key cryptography and public key based authentication protocols. The blockchain provides a common storage of the public keys and their relations and can provide the required information for the authentication process. Furthermore, the unmanned aerial vehicles store selected parts of the blockchain in order to operate independently in areas where they might not have access to the Internet. This allows unmanned aerial vehicles to authenticate entities of the network, like other unmanned aerial vehicles, cloud services, cars, and any computer.**

Keywords-unmanned aerial vehicles; flying ad-hoc networks; public key infrastructures; authentication; blockchain.

I. Introduction

Unmanned Aerial Vehicles (UAVs) have become popular recently in the civilian area because of technological advancement and their great potential for different applications. UAVs can perform a big variety of missions either controlled remotely or in an autonomous fashion. Some of the applications are, for example, delivery of goods, search and rescue missions, wildlife and terrain monitoring, providing emergency infrastructures, and many more (see, e.g., [1][2]).

The potential of the UAVs is further increased when they are forming networks to share information or to cooperate on a common mission. Due to the open nature of these networks in the civilian domain they are vulnerable to different attacks [3] and must therefore be secured properly.

In these networks, the UAVs interact with other UAVs, different kinds of vehicles, infrastructural elements, or diverse cloud services. For security in these networks, the protection goals of authenticity and integrity, among others, must be ensured. This must be ensured when UAVs provide sensor data for further processing in the cloud, for example, in the context of search and rescue missions, wildlife monitoring or collection of current weather data. The same is true in the case when cloud services supply the UAVs with data like maps, no-fly zones, proposed trajectory, or command and control data. It is, therefore, necessary to prevent UAVs and cloud services from compromising each other.

Secure communication starts with secure authentication. One important security measure is the Public Key Infrastructure (PKI), which allows the secure usage of public key cryptography. It provides the possibility to authenticate entities in a trustworthy way since it binds public keys to entities. A common approach for PKIs are hierarchical PKIs where trusted third parties guarantee the bond between public keys and entities. The trusted third parties can, however, be a single point of failure and can, hence, be considered as a weakness. Decentralized approaches like peer-to-peer PKIs are alternatives to the hierarchical PKIs. The blockchain technology has added new possibilities to design decentralized PKIs, which is why they are attractive alternatives to hierarchical PKIs.

In this paper, we propose a blockchain-based PKI for UAVs. The remainder of the paper is organized as follows: in Section II, a selection of related work is presented. Subsequently, an overview of the relevant technology is given in Section III. Further in Section IV, the design of the blockchain-based PKI is proposed. The resarch project ADACORSA is briefly introduced in Section V. Section VI concludes the paper and states what is planned in the future.

II. Related Work

Recently, different solutions for the authentication in networks of UAVs have been proposed. For example, Rodrigues et. al [4] adapted authentication protocols from the area of wireless sensor networks for the use in networks of UAVs. They use the ground control stations as trusted third parties where the UAVs are registered. Thompson and Thulasiramen [5] proposed to use symmetric key cryptography for the communication in swarms of UAVs because of the better performance. The symmetric key has to be preloaded to the UAVs before the mission and the swarm of UAVs forms a closed network.

Blockchain technology has already been used to design blockchain-based PKIs and authentication systems in different domains, including networks of UAVs. For example, Yakubov et al. use blockchain technology to improve existing PKIs systems like the peer-to-peer PKI used in PGP [6] and hierarchical PKIs based on X.509 certificates [7]. An overview of blockchain-based PKIs can be found in [8].

For example, Yazdinejad et al. [9] utilized blockchain technology to develop an authentication system for UAVs in smart cities which are divided into zones. For every zone, a zone controller is responsible and logs its activities on a public blockchain. The UAVs have to register at a zone controller.

It assigns cryptographic keys to the UAV and logs the data of the drone in the blockchain.

In this paper, we use the blockchain technology to design a decentralized PKI, i.d., trusted third parties are not required, for open networks of UAVs and the Internet of UAVs.

III. Background

In this section a short overview of the different relevant technologies is given: In Subsection III-A, the characteristcis of networks of UAVs are described. Blockchain technology is presented in Subsection III-B and PKIs and their trust models in Subsection III-C.

A. Network of UAVs

Wireless communication technology enables the UAV to communicate with different entities: with the ground station their operator, with other UAVs, with other types of vehicles, and, possibly, other services in a private or public cloud. By forming Flying Ad-hoc Networks (FANETs), UAVs can exchange information and cooperate in order to fulfill their mission. If the UAVs are connected to the Internet, their network is expanded to the Internet of UAVs as a part of the Internet of Things.

FANETs are a subset of Mobile Ad-hoc Networks (MANETs) and share some of their characteristics but also differ in some aspects. FANETs are characterized by a high mobility of their nodes, a continuously changing topology, a low node density, and limited available resources of the nodes like power, memory, and computational power. Therefore, security solutions of the MANET domain cannot be adopted without risking that they become less efficient or even fail [2].

B. Blockchain

Blockchain technology, introduced by the bitcoin protocol [10] in 2008, allows agreement on a common state of a system in an open network in a decentralized manner, i.e., without using trusted third parties or intermediaries. The term blockchain has two different but related meanings. In the first meaning, it denotes a special data structure whose elements, the blocks, are connected by cryptographic hash functions. A block consists of a block header with meta data and a list of transactions,i.e., the content. The list of transactions is cryptographically linked to the block header, e.g., by a Merkle tree [11]. In the second meaning, it describes a system in which this data structure is distributed in a (peer-to-peer) network and an associated protocol that prescribes how new data can be added and agreed upon (consensus process). The protocol allows only to append new data and it should be impossible to delete blocks that the network has agreed on. For an overview of consensus protocols we refer exemplary to [12].

One can distinguish between different kinds of blockchain systems [13]: In a public blockchain, everyone can read the stored data and can participate in the consensus process, in principle. In a consortium blockchain, a selected group is allowed to attend the consensus process. The stored data may be read by selected members or by the public. In a private blockchain, all participants belong to the same organization and the system cannot be accessed by the public.

The advantage of blockchain systems from a security point of view is that they can guarantee the integrity and availability of the stored data [8]. Since blockchain systems can be very transparent and their state can be observed and checked by the participants, they do not require much trust in each other. Therefore, it is possible to store data generated by the blockchain, e.g. blockchain tokens, in a trustworthy manner. However, additional measures must be taken to ensure that other kinds of data that does not stem from the blockchain can be trusted.

C. Public Key Infrastructures and Trust Models

PKIs allow the secure usage of public key cryptography by binding public keys to identities in a trustworthy manner [14]. Usually PKIs issue certificates which confirm that the mentioned identity controls the associated keys. Furthermore, they also manage, distribute, and sometimes revoke certificates. The trust model (or authentication metric) of the PKI defines the set of rules to accept certificates. Two classes of PKIs can be distinguish: hierarchical PKIs and peer-to-peer PKIs.

Hierarchical PKIs are categorized by the fact that only special entities, the so called Certificate Authorities (CAs) have the right to issue and revoke certificates to other entities, including other CAs. Since these CAs can also issue certificates, a hierarchy of CAs emerges. A CA which is not certified by another CA is called Root-CA and serves as a trust anchor; the other CAs are called intermediary CAs. Hence, the certified entities are connected by a chain of certificates to the Root-CA. The security of certificates (and the chain of certificates) depends on the trustworthiness of the issuing CAs and the users have to rely on CAs to carefully verify the claimed relationships between the identities and keys.

The relationships in a PKI can be mathematically modeled as a directed graph, called trust graph, where the nodes represent the entities and their public keys and the edges represent certificates between the entities. In a hierarchical PKI, the graph has the form of a tree [14]. The leaves of the tree represent the end-entities and the root of the tree represents the Root-CA and the intermediary nodes represent the intermediary CAs.

In a simple trust model the Root-CA acts as the trust anchor of the tree, i.e., all nodes directly trust the root and, hence, indirectly trust all other nodes. Even entities which are not part of the tree can decide to trust the root and, therefore, also any node of the tree. A hierarchical PKI is not limited to a single Root-CA (and a single tree), but can have several independent Root-CAs and, hence, several trust anchors. There are several methods to connect the different trees to each other, e.g., it might be sufficient that the user decides to directly trust a set of the different trust anchors. Another possibility is to introduce a new Root-CA and subordinate the existing ones. Cross certification (roots certify each other) or bridges (a new node that is cross-certified by several Root-CAs) are options without subordination [15]. In this trust model, the process of validating a key-identity-binding consists in finding a path from the entity to a trust anchor, i.e., finding a certificate chain.

In peer-to-peer PKIs, everyone has the right to issue and revoke certificates and, hence, users may directly trust each other. The graph of a peer-to-peer PKI is usually not a tree but has a more complex structure and might be better described by other network models like small world graphs or scale-free networks. The validation of a key-identity-binding requires finding a trustworthy path from the own node to the node of the communication partner. The associated trust model must contain a mechanism to evaluate the trustworthiness of a path.

For an overview of the different kinds of hierarchical and peer-to-peer trust models we refer exemplary to [14]–[18].

IV. Proposed Approach for a PKI for Network of UAVs

In this section, we propose a blockchain-based public key infrastructure for the networks of UAVs for the prupose of authentication. In Subsection IV-A the basic idea of our proposel is introduced. The different components of the system are described in the following subsections: the design of the blockchain in Subsection IV-B, the proposed trust model of the PKI in Subsection IV-C and the distribution of the data in Subsection IV-D. Finally, the authentication process is outlined in Subsection IV-E.

A. Overview

The basic concept of this approach is to store the public keys, the identities, and their trust relationships in a dedicated public blockchain. Therefore, the blockchain contains the trust graph of the PKI. For this purpose, the blockchain offers special transactions. Due to their limited resources, the UAVs do not participate as nodes in the blockchain system and do not store the whole blockchain. They store only the part of the blockchain which is relevant to them. During the authentication process the two UAVs combine their knowledge to find a trustworthy path in the trust graph. This idea is depicted in Figure 1.

B. Blockchain Design

We propose a dedicated public blockchain system, i.e., everyone is allowed to join the blockchain network to participate in the consensus process, with an appropriate consensus protocol because a dedicated blockchain system can be designed to fit the needs of a PKI. Here, we do not specify the blockchain design in detail, but we describe some elements of the system from a high-level point of view. For the sake of clarity, we assume a blockchain design that is based on the Bitcoin blockchain [10]. Therefore, its consensus protocol (e.g., Proof of Work, Proof of Stake, etc.) uses tokens as a currency to reward the nodes which participate in the process.

In a blockchain system, transactions are used to change the state of the system, e.g., adding new information, and the allowed set of transactions defines the capabilities of the system. Since we propose to use a dedicated blockchain, we can choose a set of transactions which provides the required

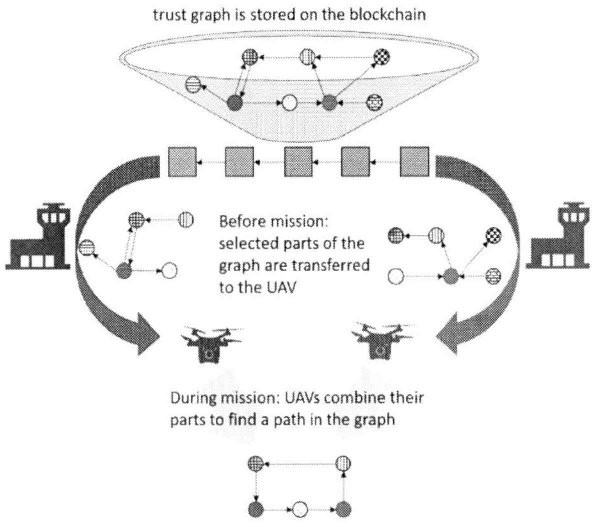

Figure 1. Schematic overview of the approach.

functionality. Therefore, the flexibility provided by transactions that allow to store and execute programs, so called smart contracts, are not needed and, hence, it is not necessary that the blockchain system offers such transactions. In contrast to the Bitcoin blockchain [10] we assume that the transactions are account-centered and do not require to reference to previous transactions and do not offer or need a scripting mechanism to release it. A transaction, therefore, usually consists of the following elements:

- A sender, i.e., the account issuing the transaction.
- A workload which contains information like the receiver of the transaction.
- Formal elements, like the type, id, hash of the transaction and cryptographic mechanisms that verify that the sender has authorized the transaction.

Since the blockchain uses tokens as currency, a transaction to create tokens, the so called coinbase transaction, and a transaction to transfer tokens are needed. Furthermore, a transaction is required to store data that represent an entity, containing its name, public key, and maybe also some of its characteristic properties like its type, model, and the responsible authority. This type of transaction creates a node of the trust graph. Transactions that confirm bindings between keys and entities fulfill the task of certificates and correspond to the creation of edges in the trust graph. The deletion of edges, i.e., the revocation of certificates, is performed by transactions that nullify previous given confirmations. These three types of transactions are sufficient to store the trust graph of a peer-to-peer PKI on the blockchain. Additional transactions can extend or optimize the functionality but are not considered here.

Furthermore, it is desirable that the blockchain system provides a secure mechanism to create checkpoints of the blockchain state. By checkpoint, we mean a data structure that stores the state of the blockchain at a given block. A checkpoint c_m at block B_m which is at the position m in the chain should have the property that the checkpoint together with the blocks $B_{m+1}, B_{m+2}, ...B_{m+n}$ is sufficient to obtain the state of the blockchain at block B_{m+n}. The checkpoint does not need to store the history of the system but only the results, e.g., it only stores the balance of an account and not changes of the balance. Therefore, a checkpoint can be used to get a compressed version of the blockchain. A checkpoint could be realized by a transaction that contains a reference to block B_m and the associated checkpoint c_m. Together with a protocol defining the creation of a checkpoint, the nodes can verify the correctness of the checkpoint and, hence, it can be used in future.

C. Trust Model

For this PKI we are using the following peer-to-peer trust model which is based on [16]: Everyone is allowed to create a transaction which binds its identity to its public keys. They can also confirm the binding between identity and public keys of other user and revoke their previous given confirmation. When a user A confirms another entity B they assign a number $n \in \{1, 2, ..., m\}$ to this relation where $m \in \mathbb{N}$ denotes a global parameter of the trust model, we write:

$$A \xrightarrow{n} B.$$

This number means the maximal length of the path starting with the edge (A, B) which the user is willing to accept: $n = 1$ means that A only trusts B; $n = 2$ that it might also trust all entities which are confirmed by B and so on. Furthermore, the path has to respect all numbers of the path, i.e., a partial path can only be as long as the number of its starting edge is allowing. For example, we evaluate the situation

$$A \xrightarrow{3} B \xrightarrow{1} C \xrightarrow{2} D.$$

Even though A accepts paths of length 3 starting with the edge (A, B), B only allows a path of length 1 starting with the edge (B, C). Therefore, the path $A - B - C - D$ is not allowed.

We have chosen this trust model since it incorporates the facts that trust is not transitive in general,

$$A \to B, B \to C \not\Rightarrow A \to C,$$

and it reduces with growing distance. Furthermore, it is simple and does not require the evaluation of parallel paths (e.g., $A - B_1 - C$ and $A - B_2 - C$) in order to determine the trustworthiness of an identity-key-binding.

D. The Data for Authentication Stored by the UAVs

The UAVs only have limited capabilities to store and process data. Therefore, the UAVs can neither participate in the blockchain network nor store the whole blockchain. They only require the nodes and edges of the trust graph they are trusting and only have to store a selection of the blockchain data, e.g., the headers of the blocks and the transactions which are relevant for their view of the trust graph. The relevant part of the trust graph may still be too big for the UAV, but it can still be reduced by the fact that every UAV has to store a part of the trust graph and can exchange their parts in the authentication process. Assuming that a node has n trusted neighbors on average, it has to store about n^m nodes and edges to reach all trusted nodes within the distance of m. But if every node stores all nodes and edges of incoming and outgoing paths of length k, which would be $2n^k$ nodes and edges, and combine its stored part with the communication partner, they can reconstruct paths of the length $2k$.

The trust graph can further be reduced by considering the trust model and by utilizing the global view on the trust graph, provided by the blockchain. Furthermore, we expect that the UAVs do not primarily confirm other UAVs, but confirm nodes representing the organization which controls the UAVs. Additionally, organizational nodes will confirm other organizational nodes, cloud services, and, therefore, the trust graph will have many hubs.

Even though there are already algorithms for distributing trust graphs (see, e.g., [19], [20]), we are still working on the development of an algorithm utilizing these aspects.

We assume that the operators or ground stations provide their UAVs with the required data before the mission and, hence, the UAV do not have to process the blockchain by themselves. Because of the limited operation time the UAVs should have a rather recent view on the trust graph during their mission.

Alternatively, the UAVs can further reduce the amount of data if it can be ensured that the UAV has access to the Internet during the whole mission. In this case they could request the required data from the blockchain network.

E. Authentication Process

Well-known public key authentication protocols can be adapted for the authentication process. We refer to [21] as an overview. Here we sketch this process from a high-level point of view: Alice and Bob are two entities (UAVs) and Alice wants to authenticate Bob.

1) Bob sends Alice a message with his identity and with a list of hashes of the nodes of his incoming paths.
2) Alice compares this list with the hashes of nodes of her outgoing paths. When she finds a common hash, she requests the data of the nodes and edges from Bob. In case she does not find a common hash, the authentication process is aborted.
3) Bob sends the requested data and Alice checks the integrity of the received data with their blockchain headers and their Merkle trees. Then, she reconstructs the path and verifies that it is valid. If one of the checks is negative, the process terminates.
4) Alice can now use the public key of Bob to authenticate Bob as prescribed in the used authentication protocol.

V. The Research Project ADACORSA

The goal of the project Airborne Data Collection on Resilient System Architectures (ADACORSA) [22] is to develop the technical components (hardware, software, etc.) to enable civilian UAVs to operate semi-autonomously beyond the visual line of sight. The project does not deal with UAVs for the military domain. To achieve this goal, work in different domains will be carried out. For example, the required electronics components for the safe and reliable flight beyond the visual line of sight will be developed, measure to increase social acceptance of civilian UAVs will be conducted. Furthermore, solutions will be designed to secure the communication of UAVs with different parties, like other UAVs, the ground stations, the operators, and other entities, especially in the area of identification and authentication. The project started in May 2020 and will last till May 2023 and brings 49 companies from different domains, research institutes and universities from 12 countries together.

VI. Conclusion and Future Work

In this paper, we have presented an approach to design a blockchain-based peer-to-peer PKI for UAVs. The blockchain serves as a secure decentralized storage for the trust graph of the PKI and grants a global view. The UAVs do not store the whole blockchain, but only parts of it and combine their knowledge of the trust graph to find a path between them.

However, here we have only specified the core concepts of such a PKI, and several steps still have to be taken: An algorithm which selects the relevant parts of the trust graph has to be developed and evaluated in an apropriate context. For this purpose, a method must be developed to generate random trust graphs. The performance of selection algorithm is then analyzed by applying it to random trust graphs of different size and structure. Subsequently, a proof of concept system must be implemented. A proof of concept system could consist of a network of single board computers, like Raspberry Pis, representing the UAVs, and more powerful computers representing ground stations and cloud services. Generally, we propose using a simple trust model which could be substituted by other ones and their performance can be compared in order to find the most appropriate one.

Acknowledgments

This work is supported by ECSEL Joint Undertaking (JU) through the Project ADACORSA under grant agreement No 876019. The JU receives support from the European Union's Horizon 2020 research and innovation programme and Germany, Netherlands, Austria, Romania, France, Sweden, Cyprus, Greece, Lithuania, Portugal, Italy, Finland, Turkey.

References

[1] H. Shakhatreh *et al.*, "Unmanned Aerial Vehicles (UAVs): A Survey on Civil Applications and Key Research Challenges," *IEEE Access*, vol. 7, pp. 48 572–48 634, 2019.

[2] I. Bekmezci, E. Sentürk, and T. Türker, "Security issues in flying ad-hoc networks (FANETs)," *Journal of Aeronautics and Space Technologies*, vol. 9, no. 2, pp. 13–21, 2016.

[3] K. Hartmann and K. Giles, "UAV exploitation: A new domain for cyber power," in *2016 8th International Conference on Cyber Conflict (CyCon)*, 2016, pp. 205–221.

[4] M. Rodrigues, J. Amaro, F. S. Osório, and B. Kalinka. R. L. J. C., "Authentication Methods for UAV Communication," in *2019 IEEE Symposium on Computers and Communications (ISCC)*, Jun. 2019, pp. 1210–1215.

[5] R. B. Thompson and P. Thulasiraman, "Confidential and authenticated communications in a large fixed-wing UAV swarm," in *2016 IEEE 15th International Symposium on Network Computing and Applications (NCA)*, Oct. 2016, pp. 375–382.

[6] A. Yakubov, W. Shbair, and R. State, "BlockPGP: A blockchain-based framework for PGP key servers," in *2018 Sixth International Symposium on Computing and Networking Workshops (CANDARW)*, 2018, pp. 316–322.

[7] A. Yakubov, W. M. Shbair, A. Wallbom, D. Sanda, and R. State, "A blockchain-based PKI management framework," in *NOMS 2018 - 2018 IEEE/IFIP Network Operations and Management Symposium*, 2018, pp. 1–6.

[8] T. Salman, M. Zolanvari, A. Erbad, R. Jain, and M. Samaka, "Security Services Using Blockchains: A State of the Art Survey," *IEEE Communications Surveys Tutorials*, vol. 21, no. 1, pp. 858–880, 2019.

[9] A. Yazdinejad *et al.*, "Enabling Drones in the Internet of Things with Decentralized Blockchain-based Security," *IEEE Internet of Things Journal*, pp. 1–1, 2020.

[10] S. Nakamoto, "Bitcoin: A peer-to-peer electronic cash system," 2008. [Online]. Available: https://bitcoin.org/bitcoin.pdf [accessed: 2021-04-01].

[11] R. C. Merkle, "A digital signature based on a conventional encryption function," in *Advances in Cryptology — CRYPTO '87*, C. Pomerance, Ed. Springer Berlin Heidelberg, 1988, pp. 369–378.

[12] G.-T. Nguyen and K. Kim, "A survey about consensus algorithms used in blockchain," *Journal of Information Processing Systems*, vol. 14, no. 1, pp. 101–128, 2018.

[13] Z. Zheng, S. Xie, H. Dai, X. Chen, and H. Wang, "An overview of blockchain technology: Architecture, consensus, and future trends," in *2017 IEEE International Congress on Big Data (BigData Congress)*, 2017, pp. 557–564.

[14] J. Buchmann, E. Karatsiolis, and A. Wiesmaier, *Introduction to Public Key Infrastructures*. Springer Berlin Heidelberg, 2013.

[15] R. Perlman, "An overview of PKI trust models," *IEEE Network*, vol. 13, no. 6, pp. 38–43, 1999.

[16] U. Maurer, "Modelling a public-key infrastructure," in *Computer Security — ESORICS 96*, ser. Lecture Notes in Computer Science, E. Bertino, H. Kurth, G. Martella, and E. Montolivo, Eds. Springer Berlin Heidelberg, 1996, pp. 325–350.

[17] M. K. Reiter and S. G. Stubblebine, "Authentication metric analysis and design," *ACM Trans. Inf. Syst. Secur.*, vol. 2, no. 2, pp. 138–158, 1999.

[18] B. Alcalde and S. Mauw, "An algebra for trust dilution and trust fusion," in *Formal Aspects in Security and Trust*, ser. Lecture Notes in Computer Science, P. Degano and J. D. Guttman, Eds. Springer Berlin Heidelberg, 2010, pp. 4–20.

[19] J.-P. Hubaux, L. Buttyán, and S. Capkun, "The Quest for Security in Mobile Ad Hoc Networks," in *Proceedings of the 2Nd ACM International Symposium on Mobile Ad Hoc Networking & Computing*, ser. MobiHoc '01. New York, NY, USA: ACM, 2001, pp. 146–155.

[20] S. Capkun, L. Buttyan, and J. Hubaux, "Self-organized public-key management for mobile ad hoc networks," *IEEE Transactions on Mobile Computing*, vol. 2, no. 1, pp. 52–64, Jan. 2003.

[21] C. Boyd and A. Mathuria, *Protocols for Authentication and Key Establishment*, ser. Information Security and Cryptography. Springer, 2003.

[22] "Adacorsa project." [Online]. Available: https://www.adacorsa.eu [accessed: 2021-04-01].

How to Prevent Misuse of IoTAG?

Bernhard Weber
Dept. Electrical Engineering and Information Technology
Ostbayerische Technische Hochschule
Regensburg, Germany
email: bernhard1.weber@st.oth-regensburg.de

Lukas Hinterberger
Dept. Mathematics and Computer Science
Freie Universität
Berlin, Germany
email: lukas.hinterberger@fu-berlin.de

Sebastian Fischer* and Rudolf Hackenberg†
Dept. Computer Science and Mathematics
Ostbayerische Technische Hochschule
Regensburg, Germany
email: sebastian.fischer@oth-regensburg.de*
rudolf.hackenberg@oth-regensburg.de†

***Abstract*—Since IoT devices are potentially insecure and offer great attack potential, in our past research we presented IoTAG, a solution where devices communicate security-related information about themselves. However, since this information can also be exploited by attackers, we present in this paper a solution against the misuse of IoTAG. In doing so, we address the two biggest problems: authentication and pairing with a trusted device. This is solved by introducing a pairing process, which uses the simultaneous authentication of equals algorithm to securely exchange and verify each others signature, and by using the server and client authentication provided by HTTP over TLS. We provide the minimum requirements and evaluate the methods used. The emphasis is on known and already proven methods. Additionally, we analyze the potential consequences of an attacker tapping the IoTAG information. Finally, we conclude that the solution successfully prevents access to IoTAG by unauthorized clients on the same network.**

Keywords*—*Internet of Things; IoTAG; device pairing; device authentication; trusted connection.

I. INTRODUCTION

As more and more devices are connected to the Internet, the so-called Internet of Things (IoT), the risk that the devices will be misused by attackers is also increasing [1]. In order to obtain an overview of one's own devices in the home network, especially in the consumer sector, we have developed the *IoT* Device IdentificAtion and RecoGnition (*IoTAG*) solution [2]. The devices provide security-relevant information about themselves to a central location (e.g., the router), which can use this information to make an analysis about security. The security analysis can be done once for each individual device and once for the complete network. IoTAG is made available to the device's network as a service which is accessible using Hypertext Transfer Protocol Secure (HTTPS) and uses the JavaScript Object Notation (JSON). IoTAG in its currently proposed version allows the access of this information by any device on the same network.

Since this information can also be useful to a potential attacker, we want to extend IoTAG so that the data is only shared between the device and a trusted central point (hub). This is to prevent an attacker from, for example, reading the firmware version of a device via IoTAG and thus finding a potential vulnerability if the firmware is no longer up to date.

In this paper we evaluate the various options for establishing a trustworthy connection that cannot be misused by a foreign device afterwards. Several aspects have to be taken into account. First, it may be possible that there is no hub in the network. In this case, the IoTAG should not be retrievable. However, if an IoTAG-capable hub is subsequently installed, it must be possible to activate it. In the second case, the IoTAG should only be read by a trusted hub. Each device must remember this hub. A subsequent change must be possible, but only with the explicit consent of the user. Otherwise, the entire mechanism is obsolete if an attacker can still find a way to get at the data.

At the end of the paper, we evaluate the risk if an attacker gets hold of the IoTAG information and what dangers result from this. If the IoTAG is used sensibly and, ideally, all devices are constantly provided with updates, then this security mechanism is not necessary, because the attacker cannot find any new attack surfaces even with the information.

The paper is structured as follows: Section II starts with the related work and similar approaches. Section III describes the security threat to our IoTAG solution. Section IV covers the solution to prevent attackers to misuse IoTAG. Section V contains the specified minimum requirements and in Section VI, we evaluate the security, if an attacker gets the IoTAG data. At the end, in Section VII, a brief conclusion is given.

II. RELATED WORK

There are already a number of approaches for implementing a pairing process between IoT devices and a central hub.

J. Han et al. propose a method that enables pairing without human intervention [3]. Instead, the recordings of multiple devices within an infrastructure are matched to ensure that the devices are in physical proximity. This approach is based on the assumption that events within the infrastructure, such as the movements of a person, can be detected by multiple devices with their respective sensors and thus the position of the device can also be determined This method assumes that the devices are physically shielded from the outside world and explicitly refers to smart home environments. It also assumes that a potential attacker has no access to this infrastructure. Since our approach is intended to enable the use of IoTAG in both industrial and private environments and both indoors and outdoors, Han et al.'s approach is not applicable.

The approach developed by X. Li et al. also relies on the combination of several sensor values to validate the pairing process [4]. The authors propose the use of wearables for this purpose. For example, when a button is pressed, it is possible to record the hand movement required for this via a smartwatch and to compare whether the button was actually pressed by the user. However, since it cannot be assumed that the end user of the IoTAG device has the necessary hardware, this approach is not suitable for use with IoTAG.

A similar approach is followed by S. Pan et al. [5]. This is based on the motion data collected by the device sensors and a camera that also evaluates these movements. This method is suitable for the use of devices that are both, portable and wireless, but not for wired or industrial devices.

III. Security Threat

IoTAG provides a network scanner with valuable information about the devices and their specifications in a IoT network. It supports the evaluation of the security of those networks, but the proposed IoTAG standard has no limitation to who could access the provided data. This allows it to be used by a variety of software programs and keeps the standard open to use for everyone. On the other hand, this could also be used by an attacker as an easy way of gaining knowledge about the targeted network and the exact devices and firmware versions used. Although, there are other relatively easy and reliable ways to accomplish that, as shown by V. Sivaraman et al. [6], this paper provides a solution to secure the IoTAG further against malicious use.

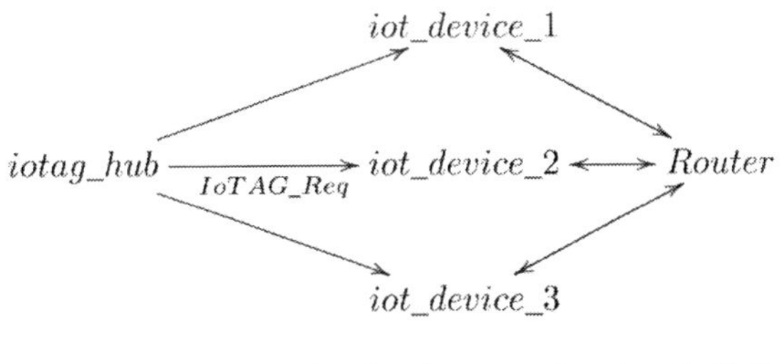

Figure 1: Example of a simple network using IoTAG.

The current published version of IoTAG has no limitation of which devices on the same network are allowed to access the device's metadata. This enables the use of IoTAG by simply scanning a network for devices which are offering the IoTAG on the specified port. Figure 1 shows a simple network topology containing IoT devices and a router, which acts as a gateway to the internet, and a device which accesses all available IoTAGs. Such a device or software is hereinafter called "IoTAG hub".

The target of the attack, which the solution proposed in this paper aims to solve, is to gain access to the IoTAG for malicious use. The attack is deemed successful if a device in the same network is able to access the meta data provided by IoTAG without the explicit permission by the network's owner. For example, a smart speaker, which is connected to the network and was programmed to collect all available IoTAGs and send them to the manufacturer for market studies, is considered malicious. In this paper we assume that the attacker already gained unrestricted access to the user's network. This, for example, could have happened by compromising an existing device, which is reachable from the internet, or by guessing or brute-forcing the pre-shared key of a wireless network. Additionally the attacker has the ability to capture all packets send over the network.

IV. Solution

To lock down the IoTAG against malicious use, its access must be limited to applications trusted by the user. This is achieved by only sending the tag to a requesting and authorized client. It splits the solution into two parts: Specifying the protocol used for authenticating a request and defining how the client gains the trust of the user and therefore gets credentials for the authentication process.

A. Authentication

For the communication with the clients, the current draft specifies the Hypertext Transfer Protocol (HTTP) over Transport Layer Security, short TLS, which combines to HTTPS (Hypertext Transfer Protocol Secure), as defined in RFC 2818 [7]. This limits the authentication to protocols which are based on HTTPS or alternatively to a self-developed protocol. As security is the main focus of this project, an own protocol is the least favorite of those option, because it would open an area for potential vulnerabilities in comparison to the use of well established and audited protocols. HTTP over TLS, as implied by the name, tunnels HTTP through a TLS encrypted connection. Both Protocols offer their own ways of authenticating a user. HTTP has two standardized ways, namely Basic Authentication and Digest Access Authentication, which are specified in the RFC 2617 [8]. The main difference is that Basic Authentication does only encode, but not encrypt, the transmitted password, while Digest Access Authentication hashes the password and, if implemented securely, also prevents replay attacks.

TLS on the other hand allows the client to provide the server with a client certificate during the handshake, as specified in RFC5246 7.4.6 [9], which allows for the authentication of the client. The client certificate has to follow the X.509 format, which is specified in RFC 5280 [10]. This format includes a signature which is unique and either signed by a trusted authority or using the certificate's private key. During the TLS handshake, the client has to proof that it holds the private key, belonging to the certificate and the server. In this case, the IoTAG service has to check if provided certificate belongs to an authorized client. This can either be achieved by maintaining a certificate authority, which signs the signature of the certificates for the allowed clients, or, if it is signed by its own private key, by validating and comparing the certificate's signature to a list of allowed signatures.

The proposed solution for IoTAG is the use of the client certificate based authentication in the TLS protocol version 1.2 or above. The devices need to offer at least the cipher suite "TLS_RSA_WITH_AES_256_CBC_SHA256" for TLS 1.2 [9] or "TLS_AES_256_GCM_SHA384" when using TLS 1.3 [11] to be future proof and to ensure that the device supports both AES-256 and SHA-256, which is used during the pairing process. The hub needs to support both TLS versions and both ciphers and ideally should also support the use of the other cipher suites specified. This option is chosen over HTTP authentication because it is implemented in the security layer itself. Basic authentication's security is purely based on the secure channel which is used for communication. A potential attacker could silently break the SSL encryption during the initial pairing, as the server certificate used by the device is unknown to the hub at this point. The credentials are transmitted without any encryption and could easily be reused, once the attacker knows them. The Digest Access Authentication on the other hand is encrypted, but the credentials need to be sent to the hub at some point during the pairing. This initial transmission could be encrypted by using an additional pairing algorithm, but this would unnecessarily complicate the process. The TLS authentication is the best fit, because the private key of both sides are never shared with anyone else and the signature can easily be saved during the pairing process and then be verified on each connection.

B. Pairing

To ensure that the client connecting to an IoT device is trusted, an initial pairing is needed. This prevents potential malicious clients to gain access to the IoTAG of a device, which otherwise could help them to get useful information for an attack (see Section VI). The pairing has two main aspects it needs to achieve: The IoTAG service on the IoT device needs to be sure that the connecting hub is trusted by the user and that the secure connection is directly between the two devices without anyone listening (man-in-the-middle). Optionally, the hub should also be able to verify, if the server is paired with the actual device.

The proposed solution for the verification of the hub is the use of a key phrase, hereinafter called PIN, which is randomly generated for authentication purposes and limiting the ability to pair with a device to specific time slots. The complexity of the PIN is chosen by the device manufacturer with minimal requirements, as stated later in this section. The generated PIN needs to be provided to the end user together with the device. For example, it could be written onto a sticker on the device itself, or it could be printed onto a piece of paper which comes in the box.

The time slot limitation can be implemented by the manufacturer in the following two ways, depending on the type of device. The first option is to give the device a physical button which needs to be pressed during the pairing process and opens the IoTAG service for new connections for a limited time. This solution works for devices that already have a button or can easily integrate one in their hardware design. This is the preferred option as it needs an explicit action done by the user, which ensures that it is the user's intention to enable IoTAG. The second option provides a way to accommodate devices where the manufacturer does not want to or can not integrate a button into the design. It allows new connections to come in for a specific amount of time after each fresh boot of the device. In both cases, the option to pair with a new hub is disabled once a client is paired to the device and can only be enabled again by a factory reset of the device. This further secures the protocol against malicious use, as it prevents any third party access to the IoTAG in an already configured environment. The exact minimum requirements are specified in Section V.

To provide the hub with a way of verifying the identity of the device, the manufacturer can provide the user with a URL pointing to the public key of a certificate authority as specified in RFC 5246 [9] and RFC 8446 [11] in the X.509 format. The given certificate authority must be the one used to sign the server certificate of the IoT device. The user can provide the hub with this URL during the pairing process, which enables the hub to verify on each connection that the certificate used by the IoT device is a genuine one and approved by the manufacturer. Alternatively, the hub could already come with a list of those certificate authorities to further ease the pairing process for the user. This step is only an additional layer of security and is not required for a secure communication, as the hub can already verify that the other device knows the PIN.

In conclusion, the proposed pairing process has the following steps: the IoT device enables the access to the IoTAG service running on it. This is either done during the boot of the device, or by a button press. In each case, the IoTAG service becomes unavailable, if no pairing is done after a specific time period. During this time slot, the device broadcasts every second a "hello"-packet to the whole network, it is connected to. The hub receives those packets and lets the user know that a new device is available for pairing. The user is then prompted to input the PIN and the hub generates and saves a new client certificate. The signature of this certificate is later encrypted and sent to the IoT device. Once the process is initiated by the user, the hub sends a "hello"-packet back to the device. This communication is done using TCP on the port 27071.

The encryption is done using the Advanced Encryption Standard (AES), as described by V. Rijmen et al. [12], using Cipher Block Chaining (CBC), as described by M. J. Dworkin et al. [13], with a random initialization vector and a key length of 256 bit. Additionally, a random sequence with the length of the key is added to the beginning of the certificate signature. This allows the IoT device to decrypt the whole signature without knowledge about the randomly generated initialization vector.

The key used for the encryption, is generated using the simultaneous authentication of equals algorithm (SAE), a password-authenticated key agreement protocol, which was developed by D. Harkins in 2008 [14] and was later updated and published as the Dragonfly Key Exchange in RFC 7664 [15]. Both, the 802.11 Wi-Fi specification by IEEE [16] and the newest Wi-Fi protected access version 3 [17], use SAE as part of their security. Due to this wide use, IoT devices should be capable of it already, or, at least have the processing resources needed for an implementation. SAE enables two devices to calculate the same, high-entropy secret, called PMK, while using a potentially low-entropy key as the shared secret. It prevents offline attacks, as the PIN cannot be guessed without contacting the device for verification, online attacks, as an attacker will not be able to guess the PIN or PMK by just observing, and replay attacks, as the knowledge of a PMK is of no use for each new pairing process. Additionally, once a hub is paired, even the knowledge of the PIN does not enable an attacker access to the IoTAG, as only one hub is allowed. Overall, the high-entropy key generated by SAE, allows the IoTAG service to use user-friendly and relatively easy keys (PIN) as a secure way to authenticate a hub. For compatibility with AES 256 and to ensure compatibility with the IoT devices, the used hash algorithm for IoTAG for SAE is set to SHA-256 [15] [16].

The key generation process for IoTAG access works as follows: if the device receives a "hello"-packet during the pairing time slot from a potential hub, it sends a SAE commit message, as specified in IEEE 802.11 [16], to the hub, which responds with his commit message. Once the device is done with the key generation, it sends the SAE confirm message to the hub, which answers with its confirm message. After receiving the message both, the hub and the device verify the validity of the calculated values and, if they are correct, the PMK is successfully determined and the hub uses this PMK as the key for the AES encryption of the signature. The whole pairing process, including the exchange of the signatures, is visualized in Figure 2.

The encrypted message containing the client certificate's signature is afterwards send to the IoT device, using the same communication channel. Once the device receives the message from the hub, it uses the previously calculated PMK to decrypt the provided signature, while also using a random initialization vector and discarding the first block after the decryption. If the message is of a valid format, the signature is saved, the pairing gets disabled and connections to the device are limited to the provided client certificate. Additionally, the device responds to the server with an encrypted message containing its certificate signature using the same PMK and procedure as described before. The hub can then verify the format and save the signature, so it can verify the device's identity later.

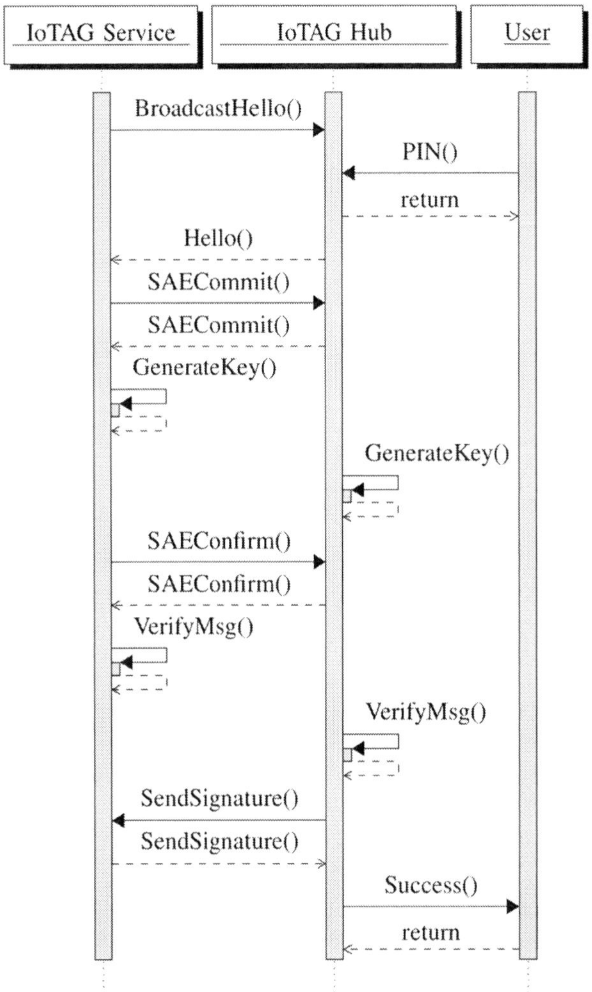

Figure 2: Pairing process between the device and the hub.

V. Specified Minimum Requirements

As a guideline for the manufactures, we define the following minimum requirements. The time slot chosen, should provide the user with enough time to comfortably configure the connection, while also providing additional security against external attacks. It should be at least 1 minute and shall not exceed 10 minutes. The manufacturer is free to choose a duration in between those limits, depending on the device type.

Concerning the security of the PIN, the following limits are specified: The PIN has to be at least decimal and 4 digits long. Alternatively it can be every other valid UTF-8 encoded string. This allows the manufacturer to use already existing unique and secret information, for example a pairing password which is used for the manufacturer's app. Also, the device needs to limit the amount of failed pairing requests to three per pairing time slot. This ensures that the average time needed for guessing the PIN using a brute-force attack is long enough

TABLE I: IOTAG DATA [18]

1	Manufacturer
2	Name
3	Serial number
4	Type
5	ID
6	Category
7	Secure boot
8	Firmware
9	Client software
10	Updates
11	Cryptography
12	Connectivity
13	Services

that its success is unrealistic, as each pairing or restart can only be initiated by the user and not by the attacker.

VI. Security Evaluation

In this section, we consider the threats in the event that an attacker can query the IoTAG information from one or all devices on the network. This means that the attacker has access to the network and is able to retrieve the IoTAG. At first, we have to look at the provided data from IoTAG (Table I). If an attacker manages to get the data from all devices, he gets a complete overview of the IoT network (provided that all devices support the IoTAG). In more detail, some information can be used to attack single devices.

A. Device Information

The device information, like manufacturer, name and serial number can be used to find existing security vulnerabilities. In addition, security vulnerabilities can also be found for other products of the manufacturer, which are often found in similar form in several products. With this information, there is no need for black box analysis. The attacker does not have to laboriously search for information about the individual devices and thus try out a device detection. With this simple information, the time required for a successful attack on individual IoT devices is reduced.

B. Software and Updates

The current software version and the update link can be used to check for outdated software. This information can also be retrieved with only the device information, but as it is presented in the IoTAG, the information can be processed automatically. This can save some time for an attacker, but the benefits for a network administrator are greater, as it provides no secret information.

C. Cryptography

The Cryptographic Information contain the concrete encryption algorithms and key lengths. This can help an attacker identify easy-to-crack methods and short key lengths. This allows the weakest device to be found specifically. This can be a huge security risk, but hiding the algorithms (security by obscurity [19]) is not the goal of encryption. The security should only be dependent on the key strength.

D. Secure boot, Connectivity and Services

Other security relevant information, like secure boot, the different connectivity and services can be used to gain more information about potential attack vectors. Most of these information are not exclusively to IoTAG and can also be found out in other ways by an attacker.

E. Evaluation

In summary, an attacker can use the IoTAG information to accelerate his attack or to find weak devices. However, the point of IoTAG is that an administrator can find the same vulnerabilities in the network and thus close the potential gaps. Thus, the advantage of IoTAG is higher than the danger that an attacker can tap the information. Furthermore, the methods presented in this paper make sure that no unauthorized entity can get access to the IoTAG.

VII. Conclusion

In its previous form, IoTAG was vulnerable to misuse by an attacker who could use it to retrieve security-critical information about the IoT devices installed in a network and thus identify the weakest point. The reason for this was the fact that the devices could not distinguish to whom they were providing this information.

This vulnerability was eliminated by the method presented in this paper. Pairing the devices with a central hub, responsible for monitoring the devices and authorized by the network operator to use the IoTAG data ensures that the devices do not respond to arbitrary requests.

The pairing is realized by the central hub transmitting the signature of a TLS certificate it has created to a device. When the HTTPS connection is established later, the client can use this signature to validate that its communication partner is the hub.

In order to create a secure communication channel between the device and the hub for the pairing process, the user stores a device-specific PIN on the hub. This PIN is used as authentication during the key exchange process, which in our case is SAE. By means of the generated key, the communication is encrypted using AES. The time factor also plays a role. The pairing process cannot be carried out at will, but is limited to a period of time predefined by the device manufacturer. This prevents an attacker from guessing the PIN and restart the pairing process.

With the completion of this work, the focus for the further development of IoTAG can now be placed on practical testing and further improvements based on the findings.

References

[1] M. Hogan and B. Piccarreta, "Interagency Report on the Status of International Cybersecurity Standardization for the Internet of Things (IoT)," Tech. rep., National Institute of Standards and Technology, 2018.

[2] L. Hinterberger, B. Weber, S. Fischer, K. Neubauer, and R. Hackenberg, "IoT Device IdentificAtion and RecoGnition (IoTAG)," CLOUD COMPUTING, 2020, p. 17, 2020.

[3] J. Han et al., "Do You Feel What I Hear? Enabling Autonomous IoT Device Pairing Using Different Sensor Types," in 2018 IEEE Symposium on Security and Privacy (SP), pp. 836–852, 2018, doi: 10.1109/SP.2018.00041.

[4] X. Li, Q. Zeng, L. Luo, and T. Luo, "T2Pair: Secure and Usable Pairing for Heterogeneous IoT Devices," in CCS '20, p. 309–323, Association for Computing Machinery, New York, NY, USA, 2020, ISBN 9781450370899, doi:10.1145/3372297.3417286.

[5] S. Pan et al., "UniverSense: IoT Device Pairing through Heterogeneous Sensing Signals," in HotMobile '18, p. 55–60, Association for Computing Machinery, New York, NY, USA, 2018, ISBN 9781450356305, doi:10.1145/3177102.3177108.

[6] V. Sivaraman, D. Chan, D. Earl, and R. Boreli, "Smart-Phones Attacking Smart-Homes," in Proceedings of the 9th ACM Conference on Security & Privacy in Wireless and Mobile Networks, WiSec '16, p. 195–200, Association for Computing Machinery, New York, NY, USA, 2016, ISBN 9781450342704, doi:10.1145/2939918.2939925.

[7] E. Rescorla, "HTTP Over TLS," RFC 2818, RFC Editor, May 2000, doi:10.17487/RFC2818.

[8] J. Franks et al., "HTTP Authentication: Basic and Digest Access Authentication," RFC 2617, RFC Editor, June 1999, doi:10.17487/RFC2617.

[9] T. Dierks and E. Rescorla, "The Transport Layer Security (TLS) Protocol Version 1.2," RFC 5246, RFC Editor, August 2008, doi: 10.17487/RFC5246.

[10] D. Cooper et al., "Internet X.509 Public Key Infrastructure Certificate and Certificate Revocation List (CRL) Profile," RFC 5280, RFC Editor, May 2008, doi:10.17487/RFC5280.

[11] E. Rescorla, "The Transport Layer Security (TLS) Protocol Version 1.3," RFC 8446, RFC Editor, August 2018, doi:10.17487/RFC8446.

[12] V. Rijmen and J. Daemen, "Advanced encryption standard," Proceedings of Federal Information Processing Standards Publications, National Institute of Standards and Technology, pp. 19–22, 2001.

[13] M. J. Dworkin, "Recommendation for Block Cipher Modes of Operation: Methods and Techniques," National Institute of Standards and Technology, 2001.

[14] D. Harkins, "Simultaneous Authentication of Equals: A Secure, Password-Based Key Exchange for Mesh Networks," in 2008 Second International Conference on Sensor Technologies and Applications (sensorcomm 2008), pp. 839–844, 2008, doi:10.1109/SENSORCOMM.2008.131.

[15] D. Harkins, "Dragonfly Key Exchange," RFC 7664, RFC Editor, November 2015, doi:10.17487/RFC7664.

[16] I. . W. Group, "IEEE Standard for Information Technology–Telecommunications and Information Exchange between Systems - Local and Metropolitan Area Networks–Specific Requirements - Part 11: Wireless LAN Medium Access Control (MAC) and Physical Layer (PHY) Specifications," IEEE Std 802.11-2020 (Revision of IEEE Std 802.11-2016), pp. 1–4379, 2021, doi:10.1109/IEEESTD.2021.9363693.

[17] Wi-Fi-Alliance, "WPA3 specification version 2.0," 2020.

[18] L. Hinterberger, S. Fischer, B. Weber, K. Neubauer, and R. Hackenberg, "Extended Definition of the Proposed Open Standard for IoT Device IdentificAtion and RecoGnition (IoTAG)," The International Journal on Advances in Internet Technology, vol. 13, pp. 110–121, 2020.

[19] R. T. Mercuri and P. Neumann, "Security by obscurity," Commun. ACM, 46, p. 160, 2003.

Incorporating Permanent Audit Trails for Corporates

Bob Duncan
Business School
University of Aberdeen
King's College, Aberdeen, UK
and
Arcada University of Applied Sciences
Jan-Magnus Janssons plats 1, 00550 Helsinki, Finland
Email:robert.duncan@abdn.ac.uk

Magnus Westerlund
and John Wickström
Department of Business Management and Analytics
Arcada University of Applied Sciences
Jan-Magnus Janssons plats 1, 00550 Helsinki, Finland
Email:magnus.westerlund@arcada.fi, wickstjo@arcada.fi

***Abstract*—All corporate businesses are under constant attack. There is no doubt that the adoption of a multitude of cheap Internet of Things devices have proved to be a great enabler of the vastly expanded potential for data collection to run systems, processes, and machines more effectively. Unfortunately, their very cheapness often means that security is not appropriately considered during design, and that the incorporation of such devices can introduce a new route in to corporate systems for attackers. The audit trail is often the single most important target for attackers to allow them to cover their tracks and remain hidden in the system for a long duration. Therefore, we must ensure we take extra precautions to properly secure this important record in a cryptographically secured immutable database, for without it, we have no means to forensically discover who has perpetrated attacks, nor how they penetrated our systems. In this paper, we explore a method of securely collecting and storing this information in an immutable database. We approach this using blockchain based smart contracts, which has the added advantage of allowing us to take a distributed approach, which also fits well with modern corporate computing infrastructures. We find that this approach can allow us to retain the relevant audit trails deemed necessary to meet corporate security goals and compliance requirements.**

Keywords*—*blockchain, IoT, smart contracts, security, audit trails

I. Introduction

The introduction of Internet of Things (IoT) devices presents a serious challenge for keeping corporate systems secure. In 2020 in the UK alone, the Government Cyber Security Breaches Survey [1] noted that almost half of all businesses suffered a breach during the previous year. In the case of large corporates, the rate of breaches was 75%. As corporate systems become ever larger and more complex, the challenge of securing them can increase exponentially. Vulnerabilities are numerous, although often well understood. However, the one area where most corporate failures lie is in the widespread inability of corporate system users to be able to retain the audit trail of key transactions processed within these highly complex information infrastructures. This is not a new problem and has been with us for a very long time.

In traditional highly centralised corporate systems, which generally used a tight firewall around all corporate IT assets within the boundaries of the organisation, attackers were still able to get in. With ever expanding corporate needs, systems have also grown and transitioned away from a centralised IT model to a more distributed approach, partly due to multiple site locations within a country, followed by multiple site locations across both other countries and indeed continents, the challenge has only intensified.

Once an attacker had successfully penetrated the system, the audit trail was often their first target, to ensure they could remove all trace of their incursion. By altering the audit trail, attackers can remove their traces so that their activities are not recognized, and their identity and localisation remains hidden, and their continued presence is guaranteed [2]. With a highly distributed network, the goal of the attacker will still be the same. The only difference will be in the exponential increase in opportunity to gain entry into a system that may struggle to maintain either physical or logical integrity.

During the past couple of decades, corporate IT systems have expanded in complexity and capability beyond all comprehension. The addition of powerful, yet cheap, IoT devices has had an impact on corporate systems and as a result may demand new forensic methods [3]. While this has allowed corporates to achieve greater cost savings, IoT gateways have opened up considerable avenues of potential access to corporate systems. Meanwhile, the appetite of attackers has merely continued to expand relentlessly year on year [4].

In this paper, we outline how we propose to tackle this serious problem with a very robust approach to resolving these difficult challenges. In Section II, we provide some background, discussing the motivation for this work, in Section III, we discuss the practical requirements for an audit trail storage solution. In Section IV, we discuss why we elected to use blockchain smart contracts to provide robust security of the audit trail records. In Section V, we outline how smart contracts can be used to deliver a persistent audit trail for corporate systems that addresses the particular weaknesses of adding IoT systems to the corporate IT systems portfolio. In Section VI, we consider how adoption of the Zero Trust approach might fit with our proposed system elements. In Section VII, we discuss our conclusions and consider future improvements and developments of this system.

II. BACKGROUND

Traditional monolithic information systems are challenging to keep secure and to retain a complete audit trail of events. When such complexities as cloud computing, IoT and distributed systems are added, the challenge grows exponentially. Duncan and Whittington [5] have written about the challenges of dealing with the proper audit of cloud systems, stressing the need to maintain a proper audit trail in these systems, and about weaknesses arising through poor configuration of database systems [6]. They proposed addressing this through the use of an immutable database to record a secure audit trail and system logging for cloud applications [7].

In this paper, we opted to avoid using traditional databases due to their mutability and subsequent unworthiness of storing something as invaluable as audit trail data. Traditional databases can be very simple to operate, store and analyse data, yet are notoriously difficult to prevent the data being modified by either internal authorized users such as administrators or by external attackers that have breached the network barrier. It is certainly the case that many early relational database management systems offered the provision of an immutable database option. The downside was that they were unable to offer the benefits of rapid searching through the use of indexed fields, thus rendering them too difficult to handle after a volume of transactions had built up. While it is certainly true that advances have since been made in more modern database systems, and the capabilities of No-SQL databases have opened up unstructured searching, nevertheless, weaknesses still remain once subject to attack.

Westerlund et al., [2] started development of a blockchain based solution for companies who wished to ensure the addition of a highly secure IoT network. Subsequent work has led to the development of a robust mechanism for a complete IoT system that can protect audit trails through the use of smart contracts as an immutable storage platform (see Subsection II-C).

A. The Audit Trail

Duncan and Whittington [8] note the huge wealth of experience accountants bring to financial systems, which have traditionally been subject to constant attack from both external and internal sources. While cash remains a highly attractive target, attackers have long realised that data often provides easier pickings. This arises because cash systems are often exceptionally well protected compared to data which can also have a significant value to an attacker.

The Oxford English Dictionary (OED) defines audit as: Audit — OED ([9]: "To make an official systematic examination of (accounts), so as to ascertain their accuracy"). This is a process (in accounting) that requires outsiders who are deemed to be both objective and expert to form their own opinion of what is being audited and to then publicly state their confidence (or otherwise) in the reliability of what they have investigated. Auditing is not straightforward or easy and a common view is that the main purpose of audit is the statutory requirement to audit financial statements. There are a further two areas in which we could find audit useful. First, IT systems audit will often be carried out in addition to financial audit, with one common weakness being that the IT system is often treated as a "black box" system, meaning too much trust may be placed in the system. IT systems audit is not mandatory, meaning many opportunities to spot weaknesses can be ignored, leaving potentially gaping security holes in systems. Second, audits are often used, as a means of assuring legislators and regulators that the legislation and regulations are being complied with. As these are often not mandatory, they tend to be carried out infrequently due to their highly sensitive nature, thus they may be contingent on a relationship between the auditor and the audited, again potentially leaving weaknesses unaddressed. However, there is a wealth of history and experience available in the accounting world that we can learn from, and in particular with our approach to improving the security of systems.

Turning to the audit trail, the OED [9] has the following two useful definitions of an audit trail: "(a) Accounting: a means of verifying the detailed transactions underlying any item in an accounting record; (b) Computing: a record of the computing processes that have been applied to a particular set of source data, showing each stage of processing and allowing the original data to be reconstituted; a record of the transactions to which a database or a file has been subjected". Thus, we can see that there is not a unified perception between the two disciplines of exactly what an audit trail is. Thus, if we accept that we can choose our own requirements to suit our purposes, we can leverage the vast wealth of audit skills and experience from the accounting world to create an accounting record that helps us adapt, improve, and satisfy our computing requirements.

In the accounting world, the audit trail provides additional information to help ensure the veracity of transactions such that in the event of a serious breach, it is possible to reconstruct what took place following examination by a forensic accountant. For our purposes, we can theoretically leverage these skills to apply this technique to any kind of data, together with verification of whatever useful information we may be seeking to retain.

Whenever a new technological area is developed, a big challenge is that it is usually difficult to find people who have the appropriate skillset — since there is a requirement for people who have both competence in audit as well as expertise in the new discipline [10]. Nevertheless, for forensic accounting purposes, a tailored audit trail that can be captured and kept fully intact, can provide copious ammunition to a forensic scientist who is called upon to investigate the aftermath of a security breach. Thus, by ensuring our audit trail provides the key evidence we require, we can significantly improve our ability to fight back against the attackers.

B. Motivation

There are a great many businesses who will only ever pay lip service to proper security [4], taking the view 'It will never happen to us' or 'We are not big enough to be of interest to attackers'. Since all business systems are under constant attack, regardless of size or annual revenue, a business should always err on the side of caution and prepare for one or more of their systems to be breached. Once that happens, there can be significant consequences. There will be the disruption of official investigations, which can drag on for months, even years, often resulting in punitive fines. The disruption of a serious breach can have a significant impact on day-to-day business, often leading to huge loss of revenue, huge reputational damage, loss of confidence in the business from customers and suppliers, as well as from stock markets, which can have a serious adverse impact on share prices. The one constant in most large breach situations is that it never ends well.

A big motivator happens on the first day of a serious breach when an attacker has taken over the systems of the business. Many companies are completely unprepared for an event such as this. At the very least, there may be significant disruption to business activities, with the extent of this depending on the nature and extent of the attack. This can turn out to be such a serious outcome that many firms have been put out of business, or caused major disruption, job losses or complete meltdowns. In the case of the EU General Data Protection Regulation (GDPR), companies have only 72 hours in which to report a breach to the regulator after detecting the event [11]. In the midst of such a panic, that would likely be far down the list of priorities, yet failure to do so would not be a valid excuse, adding to the resultant fine.

In addition, it is worth pointing out that legislators and regulators are getting ever tougher with companies who suffer major breaches, especially where they have been less than competent with their security practices. There are signs that throughout the globe, punishments are getting ever tougher, year on year. Just late last year, the Hamburg Commissioner for Data Protection and Freedom of Information fined H&M (Hennes & Mauritz) €35.3 million for data protection violations of employees' personal data. These violations only came to light when the data became accessible company wide following a misconfiguration error, following which the regulator became involved [12].

C. The IoT Secure Solution

A common challenge with distributed architectures based on cloud computing or IoT, lays in securing them. Traditionally, networks are separated into physical or logical distinct networks, but for distributed architectures we may also see overlay networks that implement certain structures on the network. These overlay networks may offer a more nuanced control over the network nodes that can include customized security protocols.

In a previous proposal, we have detailed such an approach for distributed security, whereby all entities, both actors and devices, authenticate themselves through smart contracts running on the Ethereum blockchain [13]. Further, smart contracts provide function authorization so that all entities conform to a push and pull agreement for all activities. Thus, a device owner can operate the device by executing a smart contract transaction, defined as a task, that the device listens to and then interprets into an action on the device.

This class of solutions can significantly improve the security of distributed systems as nodes can be made invisible to the network. By hardening nodes and denying any externally initiated connections to a node means that they become extremely hard to attack remotely. Although the approach still demands improvement, such as detailed event audit trails, we can foresee significant improvement for distributed systems that remain publicly hidden but whose utilization remains largely unchanged.

III. Practical Requirements for an Audit Trail Storage Solution

In this section, we discuss the requirements for an immutable, distributed, database that can hold the audit trail records in a trustworthy manner offering good redundancy. Users cannot modify or delete records from an immutable database [6] and even if the system is breached, the attacker should not be able to escalate credentials to take down the distributed database nodes [2]. Many of the early database management systems did have an immutable database option. However, there was no access to indexing, which made accessing records a slow task that would get incrementally slower the more records that were in the database. With no easy means to sort the records, analytical searches would not be an option. Without any cryptographical backing of the records, assuring the integrity of the records would also have been a difficult challenge to overcome.

The development of blockchain technology introduced novel methods of storing data in a distributed, immutable, and scalable database. Public blockchains, like Ethereum [15], provide an extremely robust mechanism to ensure the veracity of immutable transactions, albeit at a significant monetary cost, particularly for use cases such as ours. Due to this impracticality, we chose to deploy our own private blockchain by using the same toolkit that was used to create the Ethereum network.

While the Ethereum network is secure to a point of redundancy, its cryptocurrency is now so valuable that it actively attracts malicious users to explore and abuse exploits for monetary gain. The primary benefit of using a private blockchain is that it reduces the cost of operations to almost nothing, because the corporate owns the blockchain's cryptocurrency. Additionally, since the cryptocurrency's value is no-longer determined via supply and demand, attackers have significantly less to gain compared to the effort it takes to find and abuse potential vulnerabilities [14].

Database companies have slowly started proposing immutable storage systems like Amazon's Quantum Ledger Database (QLDB) [16]. This product was specifically designed for cloud applications and uses a cryptographically verifiable transaction log to ensure the integrity of transactional data, without the blockchain/smart contract transaction replication. However, since we are planning ahead to incorporate the Zero

Trust approach recommended by the NSA (see Section VI), we will not use any system based on proprietary code that is fully managed by the supplier. ImmuDB [17] has also developed a fast and cryptographically secure immutable database which can be used on conventional servers or deployed in cloud. It has arguably many improvements over the Amazon QLDB option by being open source, privately hosted, and significantly faster, but does, however, lack the built-in authorized processing of blockchain smart contracts.

IV. Why We Opted for Blockchain Technology

It is fair to say that all companies, no matter how large or small, will generally have similar incentives to ensure the completeness and veracity of their data systems. Since all companies are equally exposed to the potentially punitive levels of fines for failures to comply with the demands for increasingly tougher security and privacy requirements, all are likely to benefit from a robust approach.

In our view, the bar for corporate compliance is set to a high level so we must ensure that an exceptionally robust approach can be achieved. In addition to these stringent compliance requirements, corporate systems architectures have become so complex, that failure to secure even one small part of the system can have catastrophic consequences.

Thus, we need to ensure that every possible means should be deployed to provide an exceptionally robust method to safeguard these corporate systems. By utilizing blockchain smart contracts, we can deliver a high degree of security to all the varied and necessary audit trails, and ensure proper protection for all parts of today's highly complex systems.

It is often the case that we are faced with the task of adding huge new parts to existing complex systems, such as when we add a large IoT system to an existing corporate mega-system. There may already be some weaknesses present in many corporate systems and adding something like a large insecure IoT system brings far more risks to the equation.

It is obvious that SMEs will not have large resources at their disposal to ensure the highest security standards for their business data. Being small companies, they also have a lot to lose when anything goes wrong. In today's ever increasingly punitive jurisdictional environment, compliance failures lead to potentially massive fines, even for the minnows of the corporate world.

This paper will focus on the same approach as our IoT solution [13], which has proved to deliver the high security we sought. We can be selective about which audit trail data we seek to protect, since not every event in the main corporate systems will be critical. Naturally, all login events to access control systems will be critical to retain, as will events surrounding all financial transactions. There will be others, and the corporate can make up its own mind what needs to be secured.

While we accept that there will be a resource cost to this high security audit trail retention process, in the event of a breach, it is likely to provide more than ample reward. Currently, it is hugely challenging to understand how the attacker got in to the system and what they did once there, particularly since deleting the audit trail of their activities once in the system is their primary focus. This is why attackers are so difficult to catch.

V. How We Structured Our Approach

Having developed a working distributed security solution for IoT systems, we realised that it would be insufficient without proper attention to the main corporate system. Our current work addresses the core system into which a secure IoT system is added. The vast majority of current corporate systems are not fit for purpose as far as security is concerned. Simply bolting on a secure IoT solution still does nothing if the underlying corporate system is insecure. Thus, we were motivated to consider upcoming practices and methods to determine their potential weaknesses and to propose improved solutions.

Edge computing performs computing tasks physically close to target devices rather than on the cloud or centralised location. Edge computing offers huge potential to make it possible to apply different machine learning algorithms at the edge node. An edge computing architecture relies on pipelines crossing several security boundaries in the corporate system, but the collected data should remain on the edge node and thus privacy can be improved. Given the often distributed nature of today's large corporates, the ability to include edge computing would be a potential asset.

Machine Learning Operations (MLOps) has been proposed as a systematic software engineering method to automate and optimize AI for production [18]. MLOps looks to increase automation and improve machine learning quality in production while respecting business and regulatory requirements. It allows businesses to onboard machine learning to their operations by training, deploying, and maintaining machine learning pipelines, such as those employed for edge computing. MLOps is being proposed as an industry standard for handling operational machine learning tasks. Given that we do not intend for the audit trail data to be merely collected and safely stored, it is obvious to us that their provisions to allow for the performance of a variety of analytics on this data needs to be put in place [19], and we discuss this further in Section VII.

While we have looked at these new technologies, and are considering them for our future work, they are not specifically included in the work we have addressed in this paper. Thus, we set out to deliver an approach based on smart contracts for corporate systems that aim to utilize complex set-ups that are hard to secure with traditional physical or logical networking approaches, utilising our already proven approach to delivering robust security for IoT systems. Obviously, in this case, we would need to deliver the means to capture a variety of different audit trail data, to address whatever areas might be deemed necessary by the corporate.

Our software collects an extra copy of the data direct from every system log and audit trail source that we wish to secure and this is processed to the relevant smart contract. The multiple nodes that process the smart contracts simultaneously process this data to ensure robust security. With a multiplicity of physical locations for the nodes, we can achieve robustness, redundancy and security. The data in the blockchain is immutable, ensuring permanent security. The blockchain consensus algorithm will ensure the data is validated thus allowing us to develop trust in the data.

In the event of an attack, authorised users can access the data from the smart contract, and can compare this against the data contained in the original system logs and audit trail files, which will highlight where the attacker has attempted to cover their tracks. The necessary forensic data can be passed to the relevant authorities.

The beauty of our approach is that no major system rewrite is required to ensure that full security and privacy can be achieved. Companies are usually reticent to abandon an existing expensive system after they have added a large IoT implementation to ensure security and privacy. Rather, our approach allows us to select every part of existing and new systems to be specifically secured, without the need for major change. Since the audit trail runs concurrently with the existing system, there will be minimal disruption to existing systems, yet additional levels of security and privacy will be added.

In our initial testing, our software works exactly as planned. Processing is carried out efficiently and we can select the data we wish to inspect at will. This data extraction facility makes investigation considerably less of a challenge. Our next stage will be to set up a test server to run an example system, in which we will generate a typical selection of data. We will then carry out a range of attacks on the system to test how well the system works. We will publish the results of this investigation in due course.

VI. How this can align with the NSA Zero Trust Approach

The National Security Agency (NSA) of the US recently recommended all government, military and contractors who work for these agencies to adopt a Zero Trust strategy [20]. The essence of this approach is to assume that ALL hardware, software and people in an organisation should be regarded as having Zero Trust. On this basis, corporates will not make any weak assumptions of trust with any part of the business architecture. This paradigm shift is a very sensible and a welcome recommendation to security, but most centralized systems would need to be rebuilt from the ground up in order to comply with the ruleset.

We believe there is strong merit in adopting this approach for all corporate systems. All too often, assumptions are made about the level of trust according to hardware, software and the people in an organisation, leading to too many weaknesses in security being allowed to arise. There is no doubt that adoption of this approach will require new ways of thinking. However, if a corporate starts by adopting our secure IoT system first, this will cause no disruption to the smooth running of the business, since our IoT solution already complies with the Zero Trust model. Adopting the securing of the audit trails in the manner we suggest in this paper, will further improve security with minimal disruption.

The next stage would be to introduce the Zero Trust strategy, again in a phased way in order to minimise disruption. Once this fundamental shift in approach has been successfully carried out, we would then be ready to incorporate the next phase. Earlier in this paper, we introduced the possibility of conducting analytics on the collected data. We can foresee the possibility of using such analytics on secure data to perform all manner of useful tasks to measure the veracity of data being produced and recorded, all of which could be tailored to every single part of the business architecture of the corporate. Again, these variations could be added as required, to minimise disruption to ongoing systems.

VII. Conclusion and Future Development

In conclusion, we have developed a high security audit trail system that can theoretically be applied to protect any part of a large corporate system, which works by protecting the forensic information contained in activity logs. Since these are a frequent target of attackers, the ability to retain these records will be transformative for corporates in their fight against cyber attacks. Having the ability to identify an attack more quickly, identify how the attack was perpetrated, how it was executed, and what data was exposed will be a huge improvement when reporting to regulators. By ensuring that this data is properly encrypted in the first place and that we can identify specifically which data was compromised, and whether it was properly encrypted, the impact on personally identifiable information will be minimal, as will the resultant fine.

Furthermore, there will be an evidential trail available for authorities to follow and pursue legally, opening up the possibility that for the first time, attention will be able to have a forensic focus directed onto the criminals who perpetrated these attacks. Nation states are taking these criminal activities ever more seriously, and it will be interesting to see how criminals like having the tables turned on them for a change. Equally, it will be useful for corporates to be able to mitigate the usual massive fines that are levied against them every time they suffer a data breach.

Looking ahead to future developments, we can see that the adoption of the Zero Trust approach will remove slack perceptions of the security of corporate systems and will ensure stronger corporate systems are developed and maintained. At the same time, the ability to ensure the addition of highly secure IoT systems will provide a massive boost to security, as will be the ability to retain complete audit trails for all important corporate systems.

However, the possibility to leverage this important data that we have been able to secure will open the possibility to develop some really important capabilities. Automated analysis of server logs could provide instant feedback of an attack in process. However, it might also be possible, by developing systems using machine learning, to provide assurance of the veracity and integrity of every single element of corporate systems on an ongoing basis. Every single device, software system, server, and even the weakest link in the corporate business architecture, the people, could all be continuously monitored to ensure nothing untoward is happening.

REFERENCES

[1] HMG, "UK Cyber Security Breaches Report 2020," HMG, London, Tech. Rep., 2020. [Online]. Available: https://www.gov.uk/government/statistics/cyber-security-breaches-survey-2020 [Last access: 21 March 2021]

[2] M. Westerlund, M. Neovius, and G. Pulkkis, "Providing Tamper-Resistant Audit Trails with Distributed Ledger based Solutions for Forensics of IoT Systems using Cloud Resources," *International Journal on Advances in Security Volume 11, Number 3 & 4, 2018, pp 288 - 300*, 2018.

[3] S. Zawoad and R. Hasan, "Faiot: Towards building a forensics aware eco system for the internet of things" *2015 IEEE International Conference on Services Computing*, pp. 279-284, 2015.

[4] Verizon, "Verizon Security Breach Report 2020," Tech. Rep., 2020. [Online]. Available: https://enterprise.verizon.com/en-gb/resources/reports/dbir/ [Last access: 21 March 2021]

[5] B. Duncan and M. Whittington, "The Complexities of Auditing and Securing Systems in the Cloud — is there a Solution and will the GDPR move it up the Corporate Agenda?" *International Journal on Advances in Security*, vol. 11, no. 3&4, pp. 232–242, 2018.

[6] B. Duncan and M. Whittington, "Creating an Immutable Database for Secure Cloud Audit Trail and System Logging," *International Journal on Advances in Security*, vol. 10, no. 3&4, pp. 1–12, 2017.

[7] B. Duncan and M. Whittington, "Enhancing Cloud Security and Privacy: The Power and the Weakness of the Audit Trail," in *Cloud Computing 2016: The Seventh International Conference on Cloud Computing, GRIDs, and Virtualization*, no. April. Rome: IEEE, 2016, pp. 125–130.

[8] B. Duncan and M. Whittington, "Enhancing Cloud Security and Privacy: The Cloud Audit Problem," in *Cloud Computing 2016: The Seventh International Conference on Cloud Computing, GRIDs, and Virtualization*. Rome: IEEE, 2016, pp. 119–124.

[19] K. Grahn, M. Westerlund, and G. Pulkkis, "Analytics for network security: A survey and taxonomy", *Information fusion for cyber-security analytics*, pp. 175–193, 2017, Springer.

[9] OED, "Oxford English Dictionary," 2021. [Online]. Available: http://www.oed.com [Last access: 21 March 2021]

[10] B. Duncan and M. Whittington, "Can Forensic Audit Help Address the Cloud Forensic Problem in Light of the Requirements of the Forthcoming European Union General Data Protection Regulation?" in *Cloud Computing 2018: The Ninth International Conference on Cloud Computing, GRIDs, and Virtualization*, no. February. Barcelona, Spain: IARIA, 2018, pp. 84–89.

[11] EU, "EU General Data Protection Regulation (GDPR)," 2017. [Online]. Available: http://www.eugdpr.org/ [Last access: 21 March 2021]

[12] H. Commissioner, D. P. of Information, and Freedom, "35.3 Million Euro Fine for Data Protection Violations in H&M's Service Center," p. 1, 2020. [Online]. Available: https://datenschutz-hamburg.de/assets/pdf/2020-10-01-press-release-h+m-fine.pdf [Last access: 21 March 2021]

[13] J. Wikström, M. Westerlund, and G. Pulkkis, "Smart Contract based Distributed IoT Security: A Protocol for Autonomous Device Management," in proceedings of *21st ACM/IEEE International Symposium on Cluster, Cloud and Grid Computing (CCGrid 2021) (forthcoming)*, Melbourne, Australia, 2021 pp 1 - 6.

[14] Y. Zhao and B. Duncan, "Could Block Chain Technology Help Resolve the Cloud Forensic Problem?" in *Cloud Computing 2018: The Ninth International Conference on Cloud Computing, GRIDs, and Virtualization*, no. February. Barcelona, Spain: IARIA, 2018, pp. 39–44.

[15] V. Buterin and Others, "Ethereum white paper," *GitHub repository*, vol. 1, pp. 22–23, 2013.

[16] Amazon, "Quantum Ledger Database," 2020. [Online]. Available: https://aws.amazon.com/qldb/ [Last access: 21 March 2021]

[17] Immudb, "immudb," 2020. [Online]. Available: https://www.codenotary.com/technologies/immudb/ [Last access: 21 March 2021]

[18] E. Raj, M. Westerlund, and L. Espinosa-Leal, "Reliable Fleet Analytics for Edge IoT Solutions", in *Cloud Computing 2020: The International Conference on Cloud Computing, GRIDs, and Virtualization*, pp 65 - 62 2020.

[20] N. S. Agency, "Embracing a zero trust security model," Tech. Rep., 2020. [Online]. Available: https://media.defense.gov/2021/Feb/25/2002588479/-1/-1/0/CSI_EMBRACING_ZT_SECURITY_MODEL_UOO115131-21.PDF [Last access: 21 March 2021]

Integrity through Non-Fungible Assessments in Cloud-Based Technology Courses

Aspen Olmsted
Fisher College
Department of Computer Science, Boston, MA 02116
email: aolmsted@fisher.edu

***Abstract*— The US and world economies need more trained technical workers. These workers' demand has driven prominent private universities to create large, reduced-cost programs for graduate students. Unfortunately, less than twenty-five percent of the population has an undergraduate degree, and most do not have the pre-requisite knowledge to enter these graduate-level programs. In this paper, we look at developing an undergraduate technology program through cloud-based automatically graded labs and assessments that can guarantee the integrity and availability required to scale these programs to meet the demand for workers with these skills. We develop techniques to increase lab participation and integrity through a concept we call non-fungible labs. We also formulate testing assessments that allow each student to have a different version of the test. We provide preliminary evidence that these assessments have, in fact, increased engagement and integrity in our online sections of courses in our undergraduate Massive Open Online Courses computer science programs.**

Keywords-E-Learning; Cloud Computing; Cybersecurity; Auto-Graders

I. INTRODUCTION

Demand for Cybersecurity workers alone is estimated to increase three hundred and fifty percent between 2013 and 2021 [1]. In response, large universities have created online cybersecurity graduate programs with reduced tuition to attract adult learners. New York University (NYU) established a Cyber Fellows scholarship program that provides a 75% scholarship to all US eligible workers [2]. Georgia Institute of Technology (Georgia Tech) has created an online MS degree earned at the cost of fewer than ten thousand dollars [3]. Both of these programs are designed to scale to thousands of students. Fisher College [4] is a small minority-serving private liberal arts college located in downtown Boston, MA. At Fisher College, we have designed an undergraduate program designed to serve our students online with scalability and integrity.

Like many sciences, computer science devotes a great deal of the students' time to learning to hands-on lab activities. These labs include core application, programming, database courses, and upper-level information technology, computer science, and cybersecurity courses. In programming courses, these labs have the students write application code in the language of the course. In database courses, the students are often submitting SQL queries in response to question prompts. In information technology and cybersecurity courses, the labs are often steps taken on real systems to configure systems or eliminate vulnerabilities.

In face-to-face classes, instructors often use reverse classrooms to have hands-on time with the instructor or a Teaching Assistant (TA). When they get stuck, they can get started again quickly without a long duration between submissions. The students watch lectures, read and take quizzes at home and work on the labs to facilitate the just-in-time assistance. We show that students who learn with uninterrupted time do better in the completion of the labs.

There is often a long time between a question and submission for students in online classes and the response or feedback that allows them to continue learning in the lab. Online auto-graded systems help ensure that the student will immediately get feedback, but the student may have to wait for online office hours or a response to a forum post to continue with work. There is also a problem of ensuring integrity that the student submitting the result is the student who did the lab activities.

In this paper, we describe a technique we use in developing auto-graders that allow the student to receive feedback quicker while improving the integrity that the submitter is the author of the lab. The feedback comes in the form of auto-grader unit test results and allows for peer discussions around the assignments. The number and quality of peer discussions increased because, in some cases, each student has a unique derivate of the lab they the students are completing. We call these derivate labs non-fungible because the solutions to each lab are not mutually interchangeable. So, instead of stopping student peer communication about lab solutions, we can encourage student sharing. Students naturally want to discuss the problems when they run into issues. With fungible assessments, we discourage this. With non-fungible assessments, peer-to-peer student sharing has increased the students' understanding of the lab that cannot exist with fungible assessments.

The organization of the paper is as follows. Section II describes the related work and the limitations of current methods. In Section III, we describe the elements in the secBIML programming language. Section IV explains the auto-graders we developed for our database courses. Section V describes how we developed our auto-graders for programming courses. Section VI investigates the way we build auto-graders for upper-level computer science courses. In Section VII, we drill into the auto-graders in our cyber-security upper-level courses. Section VIII looks at our research questions and preliminary empirical data. In Section IX, we discuss early data in our work with non-fungible assessments and granularity. We conclude in Section X and discuss future work.

II. RELATED WORK

Jeffrey Ulman [2] developed an E-learning system with derivate questions. The system was called Gradiance Online

Accelerated Learning (GOAL). GOAL provided quizzes and labs for several core computer science topics, including operating systems, database design, compiler design, and computer science theory. Each course was linked to a textbook with several quizzes per chapter and sometimes a few labs. The examinations were composed of questions with separate pools of correct and incorrect answers. When students take an exam, they are presented with a multiple-choice quiz where one correct answer and several wrong answers are displayed for the student to choose the right answer. The system's standard configuration was four correct answers and eight incorrect answers—this configuration yield two hundred and twenty-four non-fungible questions per each original item in the quiz. We have used GOAL over the years in database courses and found the non-fungible quiz questions allowed them to discuss the exam without giving away the answer. The non-fungible versions of the assessment will also enable an instructor to answer a single version of an assessment as an example in an online lecture. Unfortunately, GOAL only proved derivatives in the quizzes and not in the labs. GOAL's labs were auto graded, giving students immediate feedback, but since all students worked on the same labs at home, it was hard to stop answer sharing. Our work here supplements the job done in GOAL by providing both automated grading of labs and non-fungible questions per student. It was easier for GOAL to have derivative quizzes than it was for developing the derivative labs. The GOAL system was designed to run learner self-paced entirely. Labs often lead to many students' questions, so our belief is the GOAL system did not want to tackle this challenge. Our implementation assumes some form of interaction with the instructors, TAs, or peers.

McGraw Hill [3] produces a commercial E-Learning product called SIMnet. SIMnet ambition is to teach students the skills required in the utilization of the Microsoft Office suite. SIMnet provides auto-graded labs that grade the students' submissions of database, spreadsheet, presentation, and word processing software. Students can learn the skills through online lessons that present the tasks in both reading and video format. SIMnet does protect the integrity of each student's work by inserting a unique signature into the starter file that the students download. If a student tries to upload a file with a different student's signature, the system catches the integrity violation. Either the upload is rejected, or the instructor is notified, depending on the lab configuration. Unfortunately, the labs that the students perform are not differentiated between students, so nothing stops one student from copy the work in the other students' files. Our work here improves the integrity of the students' submission by deriving a different problem per student so they cannot just copy the other student's work.

Gradescope [4] sells a commercial E-Learning product that allows instructors to scan student paper-based assignments. The grading of the paper-based assignments can then be automated through the E-Learning system. The scanning feature has driven many mathematics and science departments in universities to adopt the system. A relatively unknown function of the system is the auto-graded programming framework. Gradescope designed a system that allows a student to upload a file for an assignment. The system then spins up a Docker [5] Linux session that is configured for the task. Test cases are developed in the auto-grader configuration with specific grading weights assigned for each test. We utilize this auto-grading environment for our non-fungible SQL, Python, and C# based labs.

TABLE I. SAMPLE VALUE TEST.

Field	*Value*
Name	*Assignment 1*
Value 1	*Product_code*
Value 2	*Prodcut_name*
Value 3	*List_price*
Order	*List_price*
Derivative	*Random Row*

III. DATABASE AUTO-GRADER

The auto-grader we developed for the database courses creates a docker environment with a MySQL database running on a Linux environment. The students upload their query with a specific name: query.sql. The auto-grader then reads the metadata about the assignment to determine the

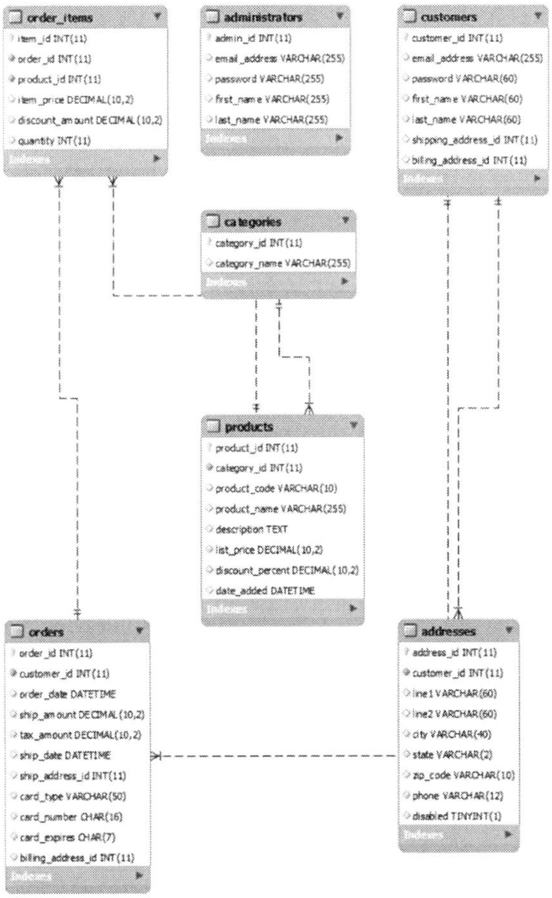

Figure 1. Student Lab ER Diagram

TABLE II. SAMPLE EXISTENCE TEST.

Field	*Value*
Name	*Assignment 2*
Test 1	*Show index from @RandomTable where key_name=@login_orders_ix*
Test 1 Type	*Exists*
Test 2	*Show index from @RandomTable where key_name=@login_orders_ix and column_name = '@RandomColumn*
Test 2 Type	*Exists*

assignment name and performs between three and five tests. Each test is weighted at two points each.

The test is actually stored in the MySQL database that is installed in the Docker session. The database connected has both the test information for the auto-graders and the same data provided to the students for their lab. There are two types of unit tests

- Value tests
- Existence tests

For the value tests, each assignment has a row in the value_unit_tests table. TABLE I shows a sample assignment row for a query that returns a specific product record. The primary key for the value_unit_test table is the name of the assignment. The value_unit_test also contains three value tests, along with an order test. The last value in the value_unit_test is the non-fungible method. Currently, supported non-fungible methods are:

- Random Row – In this non-fungible method, the student's login is converted to a unique number between 1 and the maximum assignment number. The unique number comes from an order the student id comes in the roster. The system will read the specific record in the order by value from the database to prompt the student to return that record
- Random Range – This is similar to Random Row but asks the students to return a tuple between a start and end value. The start value is the same as the random row value, and the end value is the fifth value after that record

Figure 1 shows the Entity-Relationship (ER) diagram for the student lab database. An assignment description website was built to display the question values that match the student's auto-grader tests logged in. The auto-grader will score the student on ten possible points distribute across five tests:

1. Did the query execute
2. Did the values match for the 1st value?
3. Did the values match for the 2nd value?
4. Did the values match for the 3rd value?
5. Did the order match

Existence tests are similar to value tests, except they are used to grade queries that mutate the database, such as insert, update and delete statements, and queries that create views, functions, stored procedures, and triggers. In the case of existence tests, the auto-grader will score the student on six possible points distribute across five tests:

1. Did the query execute
2. Did test 1 pass
3. Did test 2 pass

TABLE II shows an example of an entry for the existence unit test table. The case is from an assignment where the student needs to write a query to create a new index. The test types are either exists or not exists. The test will either pass or fail if there is a value returned from the query. For an exist unit test type, data should be returned for success. For not exists unit test type, no data should be returned for a successful test. Instead of a derivative based on a specific record as we used in the value unit tests, replacement variables are used to change the queries. TABLE III shows the available replacement variables. The variables allow names based on the user logged in, tables and columns to be different for each student, and literal string and numbers to randomized.

IV. PROGRAMMING AUTO-GRADER

We had previously developed a set of auto-graded foundational programming assignments in Python, Java, Visual Basic, and CSharp for students in a first programming class. Unfortunately, many of these assignments did not lend themselves to derivates that required different solutions per student. In our first attempt, we randomized the test cases to ensure students were not hard coding the output to match the input tests. To illustrate the challenge, we will itemize the labs below:

- Labs to Practice Programming Expressions:
  - Hello World – In this assignment, the student just outputs the words – Hello World.
  - Coin Counter – In this assignment, the student would be sent input variables for the number of quarters, dimes, nickels, and pennies and would

TABLE III. REPLACEMENT VARIABLES.

Variable	*Meaning*
@login	*The user code for the logged in user*
@RandomTable	*A random table from the students sample database. This variable can be suffixed with a number between 1 and 9*
@RandomColumn	*A random column from the random table selected in the variable above. This variable can be suffixed with a number between 1 and 9*
@RandomWord	*A random word from the dictionary*
@RandomInt	*A random possitive integer*

output the total in dollars and cents.

- Coin Converter – In this assignment, the students would be given dollars and cents, and they would output the minimum number of coins by denomination.
- BMI Metric – In this assignment, the student would send weight in kilograms and height in meters, and they would output the BMI.
- BMI Imperial - In this assignment, the student would be sent input of weight in pounds and height in inches, and they would output the BMI. The students would need to convert the imperial measurements to metric before calculating the BMI.
- BMI Metric with Status – This assignment is a modification of the earlier work and adds a decision branch to display Underweight, Normal, Overweight, or Obese. The students have not learned decision branching yet, so the expectation is they will use modular division for this problem.

- Labs to Practice Programming Iteration & Decision Branching:
  - Cash Register – This assignment allows multiple inputs of item prices along with a club discount card and tax rate. The student outputs the base price, price after discount, and total price.
  - Call Cost – This assignment provides the students with a rate table based on the day of week and time of day. Input is sent with the day, time, and duration of the call, and the students outputs the total cost for the request.
  - Even Numbers – This assignment has the student output a certain number of event numbers based on the number input.
  - Fibonacci - This assignment has the student produce the first n Fibonacci numbers. The number n is sent as input to the program.
- Labs to Practice Programming String Operations:
  - String Splitter – This assignment tests the student's ability to divide up an odd length input string into middle character, string up to the middle character, starting after the middle character
  - Character Type – This assignment has the student read a character of input and classify it into a lower-case letter, upper case letter, digit, or non-alphanumeric character.
- Labs to Practice Programming Functions:
  - Leap Year Function – This assignment has the student write a function that takes a parameter and return true if the year is a leap year
  - First Word Function – This assignment sends a sentence as a parameter to a function the student writes, and the student returns the first word of the sentence.
  - Remaining Word Function – This assignment sends a sentence as a parameter to a function the student writes, and the student returns the remaining words after the first word of the sentence.
- Labs to Practice Programming Lists:
  - Max in List Function – This assignment sends a list of integers as a parameter to a function the student writes, and the process should return the largest integer in the list.
  - Max Absolute in List Function – This assignment sends a list of integers as a parameter to a function the student writes. The function should return the maximum absolute value of each integer in the list.
  - Average in List Function – This assignment sends a list of integers as a parameter to a function the student writes, and the function should return the average of all the integers in the list.

A. *Non-Fungible Programming Labs*

We modified the above labs that allow students to practice programming expressions to receive a derivative version. Each of these labs initially provided the student with a formula or included an inherent method. For example, the Metric BMI lab provided students with the procedure to calculate BMI by taking the weight in kilograms and dividing by the height in meters squared. The currency-based labs used an inherent method for converting the value of each coin. For example, a nickel is worth five pennies in the US currency. We modified the labs to use different currencies or measurement systems for each student, so the calculations and currencies utilized different constants and exponents in the calculations. For example, one student would calculate the BMI using the formula of three times weight divided by two times height raised to the fourth power.

V. IT COURSE AUTO-GRADERS

This section will drill into different categories of lab auto-graders we have developed for Information Technology courses. Information Technology courses often use many tools in the labs to allow the students to understand the concepts from the lectures.

A. *Helpdesk Course Auto-graders*

In a helpdesk course, students learn technical problem-solving skills so they can solve end-user IT problems. We developed labs deployed through Docker sessions with questions and recipe-type instructions for the students to solve technical issues. We utilize the Linux Bash history file to auto-grade the student's work to ensure they execute all the recipe commands. Each student has a different user id shown in the bash prompt stored in the history file that ensured we had derivatives for each student. If a student tries to submit a file with a different prompt from the submitting student, the grader detects and rejects it.

B. *Networking Admin Course Auto-graders*

Like the helpdesk course, the networking admin course teaches the student the core competency around network tools. We developed labs utilizing Wireshark Packet Capture (PCAP) files. The students perform a network scan and then answer questions about their scan in a Google Form. They upload their PCAP file to the grader, and the grader compares the data to the form values utilizing Scapy [9]. Scapy allows the grader to parse the PCAP file and ensure that the student's form submission matches the data in their scanned file. We provide no two students submit duplicate PCAP files in two ways; the first is to ensure the timestamp is recent (within one hour of submission). We stored a CRC code for previous submissions and rejected secondary submissions that match.

VI. Computer Science Course Auto-graders

This section will drill into different categories of lab auto-graders we have developed for upper-level Computer Science courses. The upper-level computer science courses often include theory and high-level algorithms and protocols. The students need to apply these algorithms and protocols in programming labs to reinforce the ideas from the lectures.

A. *Operating Systems Auto-graders*

In an operating system course, students learn how operating systems manage limited hardware resources so that many application programs can run simultaneously. We developed auto-graders that allowed the students to explore the data structures and algorithms used to manage physical memory, virtual memory, hard disks, and the central processing unit (CPU).

B. *Networking Programming Course Auto-graders*

Students learn about the Open Systems Interconnection model (OSI) model and Transmission Control Protocol/Internet Protocol (TCP/IP) layers in a networking course. The students write programs in Python that utilize TCP/IP services that talk to a cloud application.

VII. Cybersecurity Science Course Auto-graders

This section will drill into different categories of lab auto-graders we have developed for Cybersecurity courses.

A. *Information Security Auto-graders*

Students learn about threat modeling, security policy models, access control policies, and reference monitors in an information security course. We developed a set of auto-graded reference monitor labs. The student implements a reference monitor in each lab that implements different access control policies and security policies.

B. *Secure Programming Auto-graders*

In a secure programming course, students learn how to develop code free of vulnerabilities. The perspective in a secure programming course comes from the concept that the code is a white box. The students have full visibility of the source code as they perform labs to secure the code. We developed labs where students are provided code with vulnerabilities. Docker auto-graders are provided that exploit the vulnerabilities. Students need to improve the code and submit a version without the original vulnerability to receive credit.

C. *Penetration Testing Auto-graders*

In a penetration course, students think about security from a different perspective. The perspective in a penetration testing course comes from the concept that the code is a black box. The students do not have visibility into the source code they are trying to penetrate in the labs. We developed labs where students are provided a signature for a code library with vulnerabilities. Docker auto-graders are equipped to execute the students' code and determine if they found a weakness.

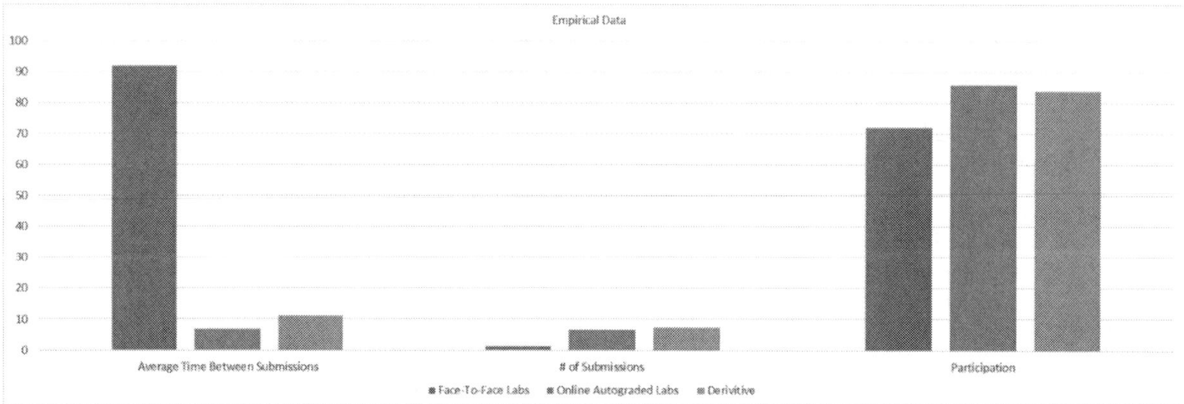

Figure 2. Empirical Data

VIII. EMPIRICAL DATA

In this section, we examine the data we gathered from three sections of a database course. There were three questions we wanted to answer about our use of auto-graders in the cybersecurity curriculum:

- Do the auto-graders help online student progress quicker through a lab
- Do the auto-graders help increase participation at the undergraduate level in labs
- Do the non-fungible assessments help students by facilitating peer discussion?

We choose the database course because every lab had a non-fungible version so that each student was working on a unique problem in the lab. The original face-to-face section used manual graded lab submissions without non-fungible derivatives, one online section used auto-graded fungible labs, and one section used non-fungible labs. The students in the face-to-face section had a reverse classroom where they worked individually on labs during class time, and the instructor would answer questions as they ran into problems. In the non-fungible labs section, a discussion forum was provided for students to complete the lab.

Figure 2 shows a summary of the data we used to answer the questions. The average time between submissions was reduced significantly for the two sections that utilized auto-graders. The number of submissions was increased for the two sections that used auto-graders. Lastly, the participation rate was raised for the two sections that used auto-graders.

The three research statements' answer was a strong yes to the first two and a weaker yes to the third question. The auto-graders helped online student progress quicker through the lab by shortening the time between submissions. The increase in submissions with the auto-graded assessments shows an increase in participation. In our small study, the auto-graders helped increase involvement at the undergraduate level in both versions of the labs. Lastly, we believe the non-fungible assessment helped students by facilitating peer discussion. The participation rate was a little lower for the derivative version of the labs. Still, we felt it was close enough to the non-derivate lab to show progress in learning since students were performing unique work, and the increased student communication help to facilitate that progress.

IX. GRANULARITY OF ASSIGNMENT AND PARTICIPATION

In this section, we examine the participation rates in the self-paced online courses. Our goal is to increase student participation in technology courses while increasing the integrity of the assessments. We offered three core technology courses through the edX [10] platform on programming, networking, and operating systems. TABLE IV shows the enrollment and completion data from the first year. The number of auditors is the number of learners who signed up for the free version of the course in the table. The free version offered the recorded lectures, readings, and discussion forums. The verified users pay a small fee for access to the assessments, course certificate, and undergraduate credits. Based on our first year of data in three foundations courses, less than half the students who took the initiative to sign up as a verified learned completed enough of the assessments to earn the course certificate and the undergraduate credits. The courses are still available for the students to complete the work, but we do not expect students who lost motivation to return.

TABLE IV. ONE YEAR STUDENT PARTICIPATION RATES

Course	*Auditors*	*Verified*	*Completed*
Programming	*39,657*	*698*	*241*
Networking	*17,671*	*743*	*273*
OS	*16,945*	*721*	*264*

In a recent experiment, we offered programming courses on the Coursera [11]. These offerings were targeted at an audience with less technical experience. In our development, we wanted to create non-fungible programming assignments and opted for smaller grained tasks than we offered in our early work. For example, if we assess a lesson on iteration, the student is given a job that has them write a loop until a condition is seen in each student's different code. These offerings are just a few months old, but preliminary data shows a much higher completion rate by the learners in these assigned.

X. CONCLUSIONS AND FUTURE WORK

Our research demonstrates that the use of our E-learning auto-graded assignments improves participation in the technology course assessments. We also show that using our technique of creating non-fungible versions of the lab for each student can increase communication between students and improve learning. Our future work will continue to develop finer-grained versions of assessments that allow for labs in the advanced courses that randomize the unit test data and provide for non-fungible assessments per student. We will also gather more empirical evidence in the future to show how the auto-graders improve the learning experience for online E-Learners.

REFERENCES

[1] S. Morgan, "Cybersecurity Talent Crunch To Create 3.5 Million Unfilled Jobs Globally By 2021," Cybercrime Magazine, 24 October 2019. [Online]. Available: https://cybersecurityventures.com/jobs/. [Accessed 8 April 2020].

[2] NYU Tandon, "NYU Cyber Fellows," 2020. [Online]. Available: https://engineering.nyu.edu/academics/programs/cybersecurity-ms-online/nyu-cyber-fellows. [Accessed 8 April 2020].

[3] Georgia Institute of Technology, "Online Master of Science in Cybersecurity," 2019. [Online]. Available: https://info.pe.gatech.edu/oms-cybersecurity/?utm_source=cpc-

google&utm_medium=paid&utm_campaign=omsc-search-converge-top5&gclid=CjwKCAjw7LX0BRBiEiwA__gNw2xT3-grxlfiyfYGdGDGIpZZSkf6_bIttgoipp830ue3le5MByUu0hoCGtoQAvD_BwE. [Accessed 8 April 2020].

[4] Fisher College, "Find the world at Fisher," 2020. [Online]. Available: www.fisher.edu. [Accessed 8 April 2020].

[5] J. D. Ullman, "Gradiance online accelerated learning," in *Proceedings of the 28th Australasian Conference on Computer Science*, Newcastle, Australia, 2005.

[6] McGraw Hill, "SIMnet," 2020. [Online]. Available: https://www.mheducation.com/highered/simnet.html. [Accessed 6 April 2020].

[7] Gradescope, "Grade All Coursework in Half the Time," 2019. [Online]. Available: https://www.gradescope.com/. [Accessed 6 April 2020].

[8] Docker Inc, "Debug your app, not your environment," 2020. [Online]. Available: https://www.docker.com/. [Accessed 6 April 2020].

[9] Philippe Biondi and the Scapy community, 2021. [Online]. Available: https://scapy.net/. [Accessed 3 February 2021].

[10] edX Inc., 2021. [Online]. Available: www.edx.org.

[11] Corsera Inc., 2021. [Online]. Available: https://www.coursera.org/. [Accessed 15 Febraury 2021].

Detecting and Identifying Fake News on Twitter

Lenna Nashif
Tandon School of Engineering
New York University
New York, USA
Email: lan9199@nyu.edu

Abstract— **This paper delves into the profound impact of social media on relaying information, which is often stored and hosted in the cloud. The ability to differentiate between correct information and information that can be termed "misinformation" or "fake news" is integral for social media platforms. The spread of misinformation can lead to severe and possibly negative effects. To understand this further, this paper uses Big Data Analytics, often applicable in cloud computing, cross-referenced with reliable newspaper sources, to understand a tweet's validity in the context of the Covid-19 pandemic. Tweepy and TextBlob are Python libraries that are used to extract, derive sentiment analysis and subjectivity, and critically analyze the data for trends and implications in tweets. This analysis then is used to locate where the misinformation is spreading from. Through rigorous testing and verification, it becomes possible to determine and indicate in a simple and effective way which tweets are reliable and which are not. Implementing cloud storage to build this out on a larger scale opens up the exciting possibility of applying this method of locating fake news on Twitter to other trending topics, including elections, scientific discussions, and sporting events.**

Keywords-social media; misinformation; Covid-19

I. INTRODUCTION

Social media is an integral part of contemporary society. Information is purveyed from one of many platforms divulging critical news at all hours of the day. This news can be coming from all corners of the globe. Such an interconnected display of communication, having brought extreme benefits, can also have downfalls. One such example is the spread of misinformation on all social media platforms, and specifically on Twitter. This misinformation ranges from harmless to very serious, with consequences that cause ripple effects worldwide. Twitter in particular is interesting to look at because it is used by so many people and is able to capture their attention in bite-sized, attention-grabbing statements. Though other social media platforms might be able to delve into the misinformation on a deeper level, users who share misinformation typically do so out of convenience rather than ill-intentions, which makes Twitter a more ideal platform to understand the phenomenon. Limiting this misinformation or identifying and indicating which tweets are incorrect can better educate users on the truth and protect them from some of the possible harms.

Current solutions tend only to determine a tweet's validity using machine learning algorithms based on engagement and comparing a tweet's contents to news articles [1]. However, controversial tweets with varying opinions can be inconclusive in many instances, causing many solutions to fail. Taking this into consideration, using a layered approach for validating tweets may be a more reliable solution. This paper proposes using a combination of *TextBlob* (a Python library for processing textual data) and *Tweepy* (a Python library that provides easy-to-use access to the Twitter API) to develop a more robust algorithm.

The paper's organization is as follows: Section II will cover additional works related to this topic. Section III presents the motivation behind this research. Section IV will further explain the technical implementation. The conclusions and possible future work close the article.

II. RELATED WORK

There are several different approaches to address the issue of false information on Twitter. One such technique is found in the study *In Detecting Fake News with Tweets' Properties* [1]. Fake news datasets were found online and were analyzed using the machine learning news classification algorithm and ensemble classification model. To understand, dissect, and evaluate the information, they used data mining to classify features related to fake news, using Decision Tree, Random Forest and Extra Tree Classifier [1]. This approach was met with success, with accuracy ranging from 99.8% to 44.15%. There was one caveat in that it maintained the assumption that the media is always the source of complete truth.

Similarly, Verma et al. [2] looked to approach this problem through the classification method. The naïve Bayes classifier and the passive-aggressive classifier were used to construct a prediction versus the actual matrix. A tweet was determined to be either real positive, false positive, false negative, or true negative. Afterward, a mathematical formula was used that calculated accuracy, precision, and recall outputting a final score for both methods. The passive-aggressive classifier itself produced 78% accuracy [2], which overall is not bad, but the final score was 50% for both scenarios, which lends more uncertainty than is desirable.

The Nikam et al. [3] work approached this differently. Each tweet that was looked into was given an individual score after comparing it to news sources [3]. Then, an overall user score was devised as a result of different conditions such as engagement and location. The two scores of the tweet and that of the user were used to create an overall score for the tweet's reputability.

III. MOTIVATION

Twitter continues to play a leading role in the worldwide dissemination of information. A great example is the 2020 US Presidential election, when Twitter began using warning labels for posts that the company believed shared false claims about the election, as well as Covid-19. Though this has not been implemented across their entire platform, there are sometimes severe consequences of showing misinformation, showing that taking proactive steps to stop this misinformation is necessary. The prevalence of Twitter use had increased throughout the Covid-19 quarantine when large numbers of people had to stay home. Twitter provided a means for socialization when other methods of interacting, primarily in-person, were limited. This increase in Twitter users brought to the forefront the necessity of having the misinformation be highlighted. Though misinformation can be harmless, sometimes the aftermath can have detrimental effects on a person's reputation, mental health, and finances [4].

Currently, Twitter has an estimated 330 million monthly active users. According to a Pew Research Center study, Twitter users tend to be younger, more likely to identify as Democrats, more highly educated, and have higher incomes than US adults overall. Most users are passive users [5], while the top 10% most prolific accounts create 80% of all content on the platform. By making the content from these active accounts more transparent, Twitter can prevent misinformation or general confusion amongst users. In this way, users can make decisions with all of the necessary information available.

IV. HYPOTHESIS AND EMPIRICAL EVIDENCE

Tweets were pulled from Twitter using Tweepy to access Twitter's API. In this case, upwards of 10K Tweets related to Covid-19 were analyzed. TextBlob's sentiment detector was used to understand the tweet's sentiment, whether positive, negative, or neutral, since misinformation is often associated with strong opinions. A tweet's overall subjectivity was also provided through TextBlob's analysis. Additionally, it is necessary to understand how a news source cited in a tweet affects reliability. By cross-referencing the cited news source with a list of already-verified resources, it is possible to reinforce if a Tweet is reliable or not. Tweets with news sources are marked in Twitter using a macro that is triggered from Python. This list was created by looking at sources that were ranked in the middle of the political spectrum so that there is little subjectivity in the reporting. For sources that are more scientific, peer-reviewed and internationally renowned sources were deemed acceptable. Included in this list is The BBC, the Associated Press, and the World Health Organizatio. This list is a continuing work, since it is possible for sources to become more or less reliable over time.

Once these two elements, tweet sentiment and news source verification, are examined, an intuitive way of seeing the tweet's validity is implemented. Bringing all of the analysis together, the tweet is marked with one of three options: a checkmark to indicate that it is likely accurate, a question mark for a tweet that requires further investigation but does not seem immediately suspicious, and a warning sign if it appears clear that there is some misinformation.

The first step in this method of understanding tweets was to connect to Twitter's API and get the dataset. Tweepy allows for tweets, retweets (including quoted retweets), favorites, replies, and followers to be extracted. Keywords related to Covid-19, such as "coronavirus", "Covid-19", and "wearamask," were used to find specific tweets. These were then run through a Python script for sentiment analysis. Additional details were surmised through Excel, and an Excel macro was created to automate the process further. The resultant information was tabulated and graphed. The list of reliable sources was cross-referenced to sources in the tweets. Cross-referencing added an element of truthfulness and reliability to them. Finally, the tweets were evaluated on whether or not both attributes were verified.

To replicate this for other topical discussions, the initital objective is to determine relevant keywords for the topic. Twitter has a list function for certain topics that can be used for this. Then, the tweets using these keywords should be pulled using Tweepy. The tweets are run through the Python code to understand sentiment and subjectivity, both key indicators of a tweets general tone and substance. If a tweet cites a news source, the news source is double-checked against a pre-defined repository of reliable sources. Lastly, the overall reliability is evaluated, based on subjectivity, sentiment, and sources. A high degree of subjectivity and strong sentiment would indicate that the tweet might not be accurate. The accuracy of the tweet is simply shown through a checkmark, a question mark, or a warning sign.

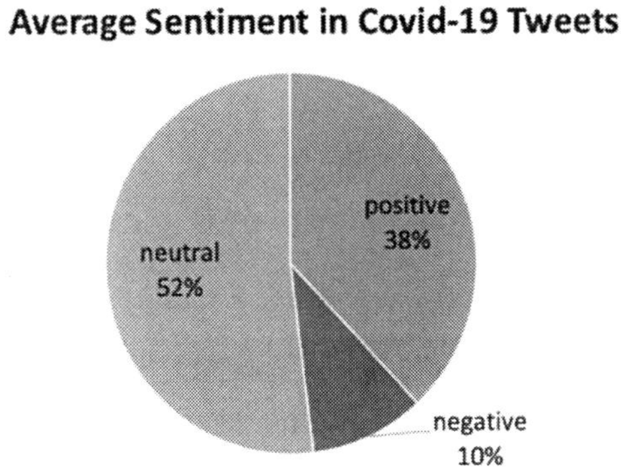

Figure 1. Results based on Textblob sentiment analysis

Figure 1 indicates the base sentiment of the tweets that were analyzed, showing that the majority of tweets, 52%, had a neutral sentiment. 38% had a positive sentiment, and only 10% of tweets regarding Covid-19 were negative.Tweets that were neutral tended to have less differentiation on whether or not they were for Covid-19 precautions. Misinformation regarding Covid-19 precautions often created divisive opinions and so being neutral showed that there was less nuance to the tweets, and therefore it was more likely to not be misinformation.

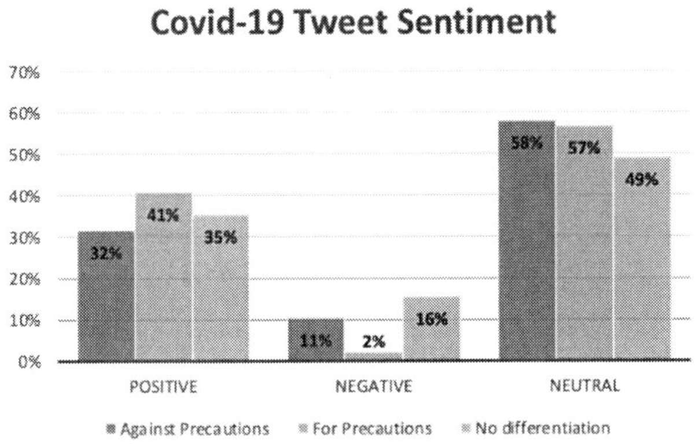

Figure 2. Additional results based on Textblob sentiment analysis.

Figure 2 delves deeper into the data shown in Figure 1. It shows that a tweet with neutral language had no clear indication of being for or against precautions. A negative tweet had a higher likelihood of being against safeguards or having no differentiation. Similarly, a tweet that was positive correlated with a greater chance of being for precautions. This can be taken a step further to say that if there is a tweet with a negative sentiment, that is against Covid-19 precautions, there is a higher chance that that tweet might have some type of misinformation

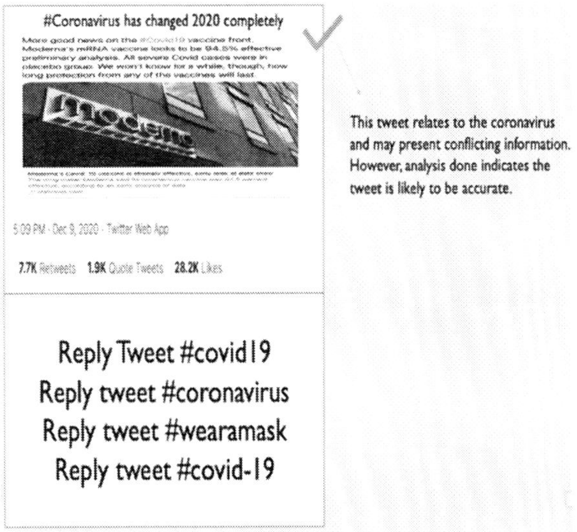

Figure 3. Sample Diagram of a Final Implementation on Twitter

Lastly, examining Figure 3 shows the finalized view on Twitter with a sample tweet that is neither for nor against precautions and citing a reliable scientific website. With the two aspects utilized, it can be confidently asserted that the tweet does not spread misinformation, as represented in the checkmark. Once a user hovers above the checkmark, there will be a blurb to explain why it is a reliable tweet.

V. Conclusion and Future Work

This paper proposed a method to bring awareness to possible Twitter misinformation based on empirical evidence, Python and Excel analysis, and the Twitter API. Tweets were evaluated to show the sentiment (positive, negative, or neutral) of a tweet that had been determined to be for or against Covid-19 precautions. Additionally, the average subjectivity for the tweets was also evaluated. Overall, the paper showed a clear method of how to identify and label a mixture of topics on Twitter as misinformation.

The efforts carried out show promising results of how to approach misinformation on Twitter. Future work will focus on cross-referencing with different news sources, additional and enhanced sentiment analysis, and analyzing larger Twitter datasets. Additionally, the current work only focused on text-based tweets, but due to the nature of Twitter, analyzing images containing text would be beneficial as well. By utilizing this method, it becomes possible to analyze tweets and data on various topics and ideas.

Acknowledgment

I would like to thank Dr. Aspen Olmsted for his support and guidance in navigating the process of writing and submitting this paper.

I would also like to thank Jason Nelson and Bansri Shah for their help in the paper-writing process.

REFERENCES

[1] N. X. Nyow and H. N. Chua, "Detecting Fake News with Tweets' Properties," 2019 IEEE Conference on Application, Information and Network Security (AINS), Pulau Pinang, Malaysia, 2019, pp. 24-29, doi: 10.1109/AINS47559.2019.8968706. [Accessed: 21-Nov-2020]

[2] P. K. Verma, V. Sharma, and S. Agarwal, "Credibility investigation for tweets and its users," 2019 3rd International Conference on Computing Methodologies and Communication (ICCMC), Erode, India, 2019, pp. 925-928, doi: 10.1109/ICCMC.2019.8819809. [Accessed: 21-Nov-2020]

[3] S. S. Nikam and R. Dalvi, "Machine Learning Algorithm based model for classification of fake news on Twitter," 2020 Fourth International Conference on I-SMAC (IoT in Social, Mobile, Analytics and Cloud) (I-SMAC), Palladam, India, 2020, pp. 1-4, doi: 10.1109/I-SMAC49090.2020.9243385. [Accessed: 21-Nov-2020]

[4] Z. Thomas, "What is the cost of 'cancel culture'?," *BBC News*, 08-Oct-2020. [Online]. Available: https://www.bbc.com/news/business-54374824. [Accessed: 23-Nov-2020].

[5] S. Wojcik and A. Hughes, "How Twitter Users Compare to the General Public," *Pew Research Center: Internet, Science & Tech*, 30-May-2020. [Online]. Available: https://www.pewresearch.org/internet/2019/04/24/sizing-up-twitter-users/. [Accessed: 23-Nov-2020]

Comparison of Benchmarks for Machine Learning Cloud Infrastructures

Manav Madan*, Christoph Reich*
Institute for Data Science, Cloud Computing and IT-Security (IDACUS)
Furtwangen University of Applied Science
Furtwangen, Germany
e-mail: {manav.madan, christoph.reich}@hs-furtwangen.de

***Abstract*—Training of neural networks requires often high computational power and large memory on Graphics Processing Unit (GPU) hardware. Many cloud providers such as Amazon, Azure, Google, Siemens, etc, provide such infrastructure. However, should one choose a cloud infrastructure or an on-premise system for a neural network application, how can these systems be compared with one another? This paper investigates seven prominent Machine Learning benchmarks, which are MLPerf, DAWNBench, DeepBench, DLBS, TBD, AIBench, and ADABench. The recent popularity and widespread use of Deep Learning in various applications have created a need for benchmarking in this field. This paper shows that these application domains need slightly different resources and argue that there is no standard benchmark suite available that addresses these different application needs. We compare these benchmarks and summarize benchmark-related datasets, domains, and metrics. Finally, a concept of an ideal benchmark is sketched.**

***Index Terms*—Machine Learning, Machine Learning Benchmark, MLPerf, AIBench, Deep learning, Survey**

I. INTRODUCTION

Training of neural networks requires high computational power and large memory. Graphics Processing Units (GPUs) can significantly speed up the training process for many Deep Learning models. Training models for tasks such as Image classification, Video analysis, and Natural language processing involve computationally intensive matrix multiplications and other operations that can take advantage of a GPU's massively parallel architecture. It can take days to train a Deep Learning model that performs intensive computational tasks with large datasets on a single processor. However, if the program is designed to transfer these tasks to one or more GPUs then the training time is reduced to a few hours instead of a few days. Many cloud providers such as Amazon, Azure, Google, Siemens, etc, are providing such infrastructures. These hardware resources vary in terms of memory, storage, and processing power capacity. On these cloud platforms, one can acquire the required resources. The question is, which fits best to the specific machine learning application. Benchmarks can help to compare these cloud infrastructures.

A benchmark is defined as either an individual program or a set of programs that measure systems performance with respect to a reference [1]. In order to use a benchmark, one has to run the individual program or the set of programs on the target machine which would generate a report characterizing the performance of the System Under Test (SUT). In terms of a computer, this performance could be related to I/O processing, running a graphics application, solving some linear equations, etc. A benchmark usually consists of four parts, which are scenario, evaluation criteria, evaluation metrics, and benchmarking score [1]. The scenario provides a detailed description of the setup environment. Evaluation criteria define important rules that specify the requirements which should be met to use the benchmark successfully. A metric quantifies a specific quality of the SUT which is the focus of the benchmark. Finally, the benchmarking score is a numerical value given to the SUT, which quantifies how well it performed according to the metric and through this numerical value one can compare the SUT with other similar systems.

A benchmark suite is defined as a collection of individual programs that help in comparing two systems or algorithms with each other. Benchmarking hardware and software provide a better understanding of the application for which they are designed and they also help to improve overall system's quality by measuring performance and highlighting bottlenecks in key areas. The past demonstrates that benchmarks have usually accelerated progress in their respective field [2]. Benchmarking is also of uttermost importance for the field of Machine Learning (ML) (with ML we imply both machine and deep learning) as with great pace new algorithms and specialized hardware are being introduced. With no standardized set of rules to compare these advancements, this might eventually slow the progress in this field. To keep up with the rapidly evolving field of ML, hardware and software vendors are coming up with specialized solutions focusing only on this domain [3]. To encourage further advancements more benchmarking tools are needed for these workloads. This paper aims to provide a comparison between seven ML benchmarks, which are MLPerf [4], DAWNBench [5], DeepBench [6], DLBS [7], TBD [8], AIBench [9], and ADABench [10] to make it easier for the new users to select the most optimal one as per their needs. These benchmarks are designed for specific applications and have their advantages and disadvantages. According to our knowledge, no effort to date has been done to compare all of these. The rest of this paper is structured as follows: we summarize related work in Section II. In Section III, we explain benchmarking from the ML perspective and list all the metrics and datasets that are usually employed by different benchmarks. Seven individual benchmarks found in the literature are presented in Section IV. In Section V, we compare these seven benchmarks and provide a thorough summary. In section VI, we reflect on the points that are lacking in current benchmark suites before concluding in Section VII.

II. RELATED WORK

As many benchmarks already exist for characterizing modern computer systems, we provide a brief overview of two such benchmarks that resulted in breakthroughs in microprocessors and hardware design [2]. First, the Systems Performance Evaluation Cooperative (SPEC) [11] benchmark. SPEC was founded in 1988 as a non-profit consortium of major computer vendors to provide an effective and fair comparison of advanced high-performance computing systems. Benchmark consisted of a set of programs (individual application benchmarks) where each carries equal weightage [12]. Second, the LINPACK benchmark [13] by Jack Dongarra, first introduced back in 1976. LINPACK comes under the category of an algorithmic benchmark that measures the floating-point performance of computers. It consists of subroutines that aim to solve a system of linear equations [12].

These benchmarks aimed to judge the relative performance of the hardware under test compared to some predefined system used as a reference. In the case of the LINPACK benchmark, the aim might be to know which microprocessor is the fastest, and generally a processor with a higher core count and a faster clock speed will outperform the others. ML workloads lack this simplicity. These workloads often utilize much complex hardware systems and algorithms which ultimately make benchmarking a difficult task [14]. This is enlightened in the third chapter. As new domains adopt ML in their life cycle, there is a constant need for benchmarking tools to evaluate different algorithms and hardware platforms to encourage further advancements.

There have been some efforts in summarizing different benchmarking principles for ML [14] but a thorough comparison between benchmarking suites is still missing. In addition to this, most available ML benchmarks do not utilize any real-world datasets that represent today's industrial need. For example, Mattson et al. [4], Zhu et al. [8], Gao et al. [9] all use ImageNet dataset [15] for benchmarking the computer vision domain but ImageNet might not be a good choice anymore for comparing Image classification [16]. Therefore in this paper, we provide a summary of commonly used benchmarks with their use cases and metrics to enlighten the fact that none of the benchmarks are completely fulfilling the industrial need.

III. BENCHMARKS FOR MACHINE LEARNING INFRASTRUCTURES

In this section, we introduce benchmarking from an ML perspective.

A. Benchmarking for ML Training and Inference

Benchmarking is a way to recognize the particular qualities and shortcomings of various approaches and frameworks. In ML, it can be associated with two individual tasks of the ML workflow, which do not overlap with each other. a) *Training:* For training an ML model, learnable parameters of the model have to be updated. This requires a forward and a backward pass wherein forward pass samples in mini-batches are shown to the model. In backward pass, intermediate results are stored in the memory which eventually adds a significant load on the hardware accelerators (usually GPUs). b) *Inference:* On the other hand, the inference is about evaluating a single data sample on the trained model at once. Therefore training usually requires expensive hardware with multiple cores whereas inference can be conducted even on simpler edge devices.

These two distinct processes have their separate benchmarks. In this paper, we focus mainly on training benchmarks as training is usually a resource expensive process. Training benchmarks compare different software solutions for a given task (e.g., Image classification) to know which one performs the best according to a particular metric. From a hardware perspective, training benchmarks focus on evaluating how fast a particular system can train a model to reach some predefined state-of-art performance for a given task. The inference benchmarks usually measure latency that translates to how fast a system can produce results in production once it has been trained.

B. Uniqueness of Machine and Deep Learning

Benchmark suites like SPEC [11] have established themselves as a source of guidance that has helped in standardizing requirements in the field of computing. Such benchmarks were successful, because of an end-to-end approach followed by the benchmark and also because of the lack of stochasticity involved in the domain [4]. ML on the other hand does not follow a common recipe. Even two runs of the same model under the same setting can produce different results [4]. Another source of randomness is the software frameworks in which the Ml model is built. In recent years there have been many such mathematical libraries that are capable of implementing a model in different ways.

The stochasticity involved in ML emerges as a major challenge when it comes to benchmarking with respect to training. This aspect is unique to ML training and is not encountered in traditional computing. ML is capable of offering multiple correct solutions for a single problem, unlike traditional technologies that offer only one perfect solution [4]. The other aspect of ML that makes benchmarking even harder is the diversity of problems that are present in the field. For example, it is not necessarily true that a system capable of solving Computer vision tasks efficiently will also be efficient for Natural language processing (NLP). Therefore, a training benchmark should aim to provide a standard evaluation criterion that considers different trade-offs (for e.g., performance vs speed vs different domains) when comparing systems or algorithms together.

Some of the requirements that an ML training benchmark should fulfill are:

- Provide a fair comparison between hardware systems and algorithms on common domains and datasets.
- Provide a fair comparison between different ML frameworks (for e.g., PyTorch vs TensorFlow) when running the same algorithm for a particular domain.
- Standardize a set of rules which could be followed by the user to ensure reproducibility of results.

- Provide a quantitative analysis between system level operations (for e.g., convolution, pooling) to know where the bottlenecks are present.
- Should measure systems on the basis of scalability (one server vs multiple servers) and should ensure transparency by using adequate metrics for each domain respectively.
- Should be able to especially handle stochasticity involved in machine learning workloads. One way of doing this to chose a metric that is consistent with the number of runs on average.
- Should be representative of industrial needs as many benchmarks in literature use datasets that are far too simple for the domain they represent.
- Should be transparent that providers of hardware or infrastructure accepting the benchmark
- Should be open source that everyone can validate the correctness of the implementation.

C. Classifications of ML/DL Benchmarks

An ML benchmark can also be categorized into one of three levels shown in Figure 1.

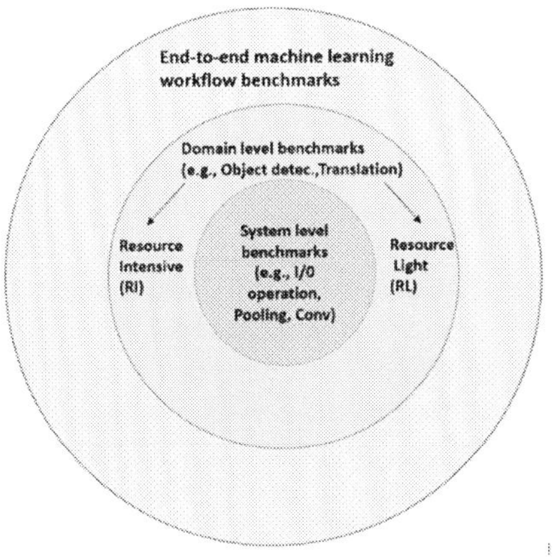

Figure 1. Category of ML benchmarks.

The first category, the *System Level (SL) benchmark* represents the lowest level, the fundament of the whole benchmarking chain. These benchmarks help to gather more insights at a basic level such that bottlenecks involved in basic operations could be found. One noteworthy example of such an operation is the activation functions involved in ML. Coleman et al. [17] showed that the rectified linear units (ReLU) [18] activation function in particular is an expensive operation prolonging the overall training process.

The second category, the *Domain level (DL) benchmark* targets specific domains that can utilize different small scale operations mentioned above. These benchmarks are important for evaluating hardware and software from a broader perspective to reflect upon the memory and computation requirements needed for each domain respectively. They are subdivided into two categories namely, **Resource Intensive (RI)** and **Resource Light (RL)**. A domain such as Image classification belong to the **Resource Intensive** subcategory, as it requires high GPU and memory whereas NLP comes under **Resource Light** subcategory due to reduced memory requirement. All of the commonly found ML benchmarks in the literature belong to the *Domain Level* benchmark category. It is important to note that these benchmarks still target only a handful of domains and also not all the domains are targeted in all of the commonly used benchmarks.

The last category, *End-to-end machine learning workflow benchmarks* focus on evaluating systems from an end to end perspective. Such benchmarks consider the whole benchmark as loosely coupled modules that could be easily changed and extended. These modules include data pre-processing pipeline, data input pipeline, different domain-specific set of operations (Domain level benchmarks), inference, training, model serving, and finally important non-artificial intelligence (AI) related modules which are critical for the application in focus. Such benchmarks provide extensive information about the SUT from training to production. In literature, AIBench Benchmark [9] is one of the few benchmark suites that comes under this category. They define this benchmark suite as a combination of essential attributes extracted out of different industry-scale applications. These particular applications define at first hand that which of the Domain level benchmarks should be used for that particular use case.

D. Metrics for ML-Benchmark

A typical ML workflow starts by gathering more insights about the data and problem at hand. This is followed by dataset formation and algorithm selection. The next step is to evaluate how well the algorithm performs and this is evaluated based on a specific metric. For example, in the task of binary classification, classification accuracy defines the fraction of samples in the test set that were predicted correctly. Using the only accuracy could be misleading due to the fact that this metric does not consider scenarios such as class imbalance. Similarly, in the case of benchmarking there are several metrics that can be employed. Choosing one over the other should be done carefully as this could be domain-specific or problem-specific. Table I provides a list of such metrics that are most commonly used by some of the machine learning benchmarks. It is important to note that most of the benchmarks chose one or two out of all the mentioned metrics.

The most commonly adopted metric out of all the above-mentioned ones is Time-to-Accuracy (TTA) metric. Coleman et al. [17] show that this metric generalizes nearly as well on unseen data. They also portray that even with all the stochasticity involved in the training procedure, the TTA metric stabilizes well with a low coefficient of variation (he ratio of the variance to the mean) concluded after multiple iterations.

E. Benchmark Datasets

A dataset is also a principal part of an ML benchmark as they help to test the system from the domain-specific

TABLE I
THE DIFFERENT METRICS THAT ARE USED BY TRAINING BENCHMARKS FOR COMPARING DIFFERENT SYSTEMS OR ALGORITHMS.

Name	Definition
TTA	*Time To Accuracy*: This metric measures the time (in seconds) to reach the predefined accuracy on validation set. The task and the algorithm are fixed during TTA measurement.
TTE	*Time To Epochs*: This metric measures the wall clock time (in seconds) taken to train some specific predefined epochs. The task and the algorithm are fixed during TTA measurement.
Energy Consumption	Energy consumed (in watts per second) till some accuracy is reached on the validation set.
Accuracy	This metric is used to compare novel algorithms with the state-of-the-art algorithms on a fixed task and a dataset in order to improve the best known results. It is defined as the number of correctly predicted samples out of the total samples present in the test set.
Cost	This metric is associated with instances in a cloud infrastructure. It describes the cost (in some currency) required for the training of an algorithm to reach a specified accuracy on validation set.
Throughput	Throughput defines the number of data points present in the training set that are processed per second on a system.
Batch time	It is the average time taken in ms to process one batch of data, i.e., the number of samples before the model is updated.
Flops	This metric measures either the floating point operations required for a particular operation (like convolution in convolutional neural networks (CNN)) or the total number of operations executed in whole training process.
GPU utilization	Fraction of time (in ms) the GPU is active in whole training process.
CPU utilization	This metric measures the average utilization of central processing unit (CPU) across all cores.
Memory Consumption	This metric aims to examine which of the operations or components utilize most of the memory. This will help in optimizing the training process.
Total time per operation	This metric calculates the time (in ms) required to complete a particular operation (convolution, pooling, etc.).

point. Mostly standard open-sourced datasets are used by the majority of benchmark suites. Each dataset reflects the targeted domain. The table below provides a summary of such datasets with information about the domain they target.

IV. ML BENCHMARKING SUITS

In this section, we summarize seven different machine and deep learning benchmarks that have emerged in past as a joint effort from academia and industry to standardize benchmarking.

A. MLPerf

MLPerf is a consortium of commercial and academic organizations that has emerged as an industry standard for measuring ML systems. It offers both training and inference benchmark suites. The training benchmark suite (version 0.7) is a collection of eight machine learning models from 6 different domains. In the current version 0.7, there are two different sets of benchmark suites where one targets regular systems and the other is for High-Performance Computing (HPC) systems. It is the first benchmarking effort that aims to provide fair evaluations of training and inference performance for hardware, software, and services under prescribed conditions that guarantee reproducibility. There are two divisions; open and closed, where different vendors can submit their results. The goal of the closed division is to do a one-to-one comparison between hardware platforms or software frameworks. To use the closed division one has to utilize the same model and optimizer provided in the reference implementation. This forces one to follow certain guidelines under which the same preprocessing steps, same model, and training method should be used. On the other hand, the open division is for encouraging further advancements by allowing arbitrary preprocessing steps, new models, and training methods [4]. This benchmark can be considered as a combination of multiple Domain level benchmarks.

TABLE II
SOME COMMON DATASETS THAT ARE USED BY TRAINING BENCHMARKS FOR COMPARING DIFFERENT SYSTEMS OR ALGORITHMS.

Name	Characteristics	Domain
ImageNet [15] Cifar10 [19]	Imagenet: close to 1.2 million images, 1000 clases in total. Cifar10: 6000 images (32*32) per class, 10 classes in total. classes in total.	Image classification
COCO [20] Pascal VOC2007 [21]	COCO: more than 2M (5 captions per image) instances in 80 object categories. Pascal VOC: 9963 images, with each image containing set of objects from 20 different classes.	Object detection.
WMT English-German [22]	Translation dataset based on the data from statmt.org.	Language Translation
1TB ClickLogs [23]	Contains instances of feature values and click feedback for millions of display ads divided into 24 files.	Recommendation
Go [4]	MiniGo, data is generated while self-playing on a 9×9 game board.	Reinforcement learning
SQuAD [24]	Close to 10k instances of questions and answers.	Question Answering
LibriSpeech [25]	Contains approximately 1000 hours of English speech with a sampling rate of 16 kHz.	Speech recognition

B. DAWNBench

DAWNBench benchmark suite can be regarded as a predecessor of MLPerf. It was designed for measuring end-to-end ML training and inference tasks. DAWNBench was introduced in November 2017 as a benchmark and a competition. Similar to MLPerf, DAWNBench also provides a reference set of common ML workloads. This benchmark was the first to use the Time-to-Accuracy (TTA) metric to measure performance and allowed users to optimize model architectures, optimization algorithms, software frameworks, and hardware platforms. But it lacked rules, i.e., closed division in comparison to MLPerf [17]. Similar to MLPerf this benchmark suite can also be considered as a collection of the Domain level benchmarks.

C. DeepBench

DeepBench was released in 2016 from the Baidu research group. It is an open-sourced benchmarking tool focused on measuring the performance of the hardware at the kernel level. It can be considered as a System level benchmark. It aims to find which basic operations involved in deep neural network training are most time-consuming. The initial release only focused on benchmarking only training performance across multiple hardware platforms but the new version includes inference also. The benchmarking tool is available as a Github repository with reference implementations [6].

D. DLBS

Published in 2017, Deep Learning Benchmarking Suite (DLBS) is part of a large, comprehensive set of tools known as HPE's Deep Learning Cookbook. The cookbook aims to provide a guide for choosing ideal hardware and software for DL for both training and inference. It contains a web-based tool for analyzing the performance of deep neural networks, a benchmark suite that is available freely on Github, and reference designs for some selected workloads. The benchmarking suite itself consists of command-line programs that run different domain specific neural networks in multiple frameworks. The results for various hardware platforms, frameworks, and models are available online. Besides, the benchmark suite is also capable of producing results for untested hardware. Another interesting point about this benchmark is that it allows user-specific customized datasets, and one can use a synthetic dataset if no dataset is available [7]. This benchmarks suite also comes under the category of Domain level benchmark.

E. TBD

TBD (TrainingBenchmark for DNNs) benchmark suite is a joint effort from EcoSystem Research Group at the University of Toronto and Project Fiddle at Microsoft Research, Redmond. The benchmark suite was first introduced in 2018 with memory profiling tools for interpreting memory bottlenecks across three frameworks (CNTK, TensorFlow, MXNET) and recommendations for hardware and software selection for deep learning training. The suite consists of eight DNN models that overall cover six major domains. It is also a combination of Domain level benchmarks.

F. AIBench

AIBench, a Datacenter AI benchmark suite is one of the benchmark that comes under the category of End-to-end machine learning workflow benchmark. It consists of 17 Domain level benchmarks and 14 System level benchmarks that target nine real-world applications with 17 AI domains. The benchmark suite consists of loosely coupled modules that are flexible and easily configurable for multiple applications. Currently, two workflows are covered by the benchmark suite, first the E-commerce Search Intelligence, and second the Online Translation Intelligence [26].

G. ADABench

ADABench Is another benchmark suite that comes under the category of End-to-end machine learning workflow benchmark. It focuses on the complete end-to-end pipeline of ML workloads that comprises several additional steps including training, data integration (data input pipeline), data cleaning (data preprocessing pipeline), feature extraction, and model serving. There is no open-sourced implementation available for this benchmark but it is one of the benchmark suites that target industry-relevant domains like predictive maintenance as one of their use cases [10].

V. COMPARISON

Table III provides a summary of benchmarks mentioned in the previous section. The columns represent (from left to right), the name of the benchmark, the datasets used by these benchmarks, domains that the benchmark suite target with their category where SL, DL (RI & RL), and E represents System level, Domain level, and End-to-end machine learning workflow benchmark, and finally the metrics these benchmark's use. Starting with MLPerf, this benchmark suite uses a single metric, i.e., TTA, and targets only a few domains (6 vs. 17 in AIBench). TTA might be a good metric for IT-companies, which have abundant hardware resources to spare, and the cost of running these models not being a critical factor. But for some, cost as a metric could be a decisive factor in determining what kind of cloud infrastructure they want to invest in. Contrarily, DAWNBench uses cost as a metric in addition to TTA but targets only two domains. Coming to DeepBench, the micro-benchmark suite uses Teraflops and total time per execution of operations as metrics. This benchmark suite covers only a small set of operations that are involved in DL training.

From Table III, we can also see that only the DLBS benchmark offers the use of user provided datasets but on the other hand it only target two domains i.e. Language translation and Image classification. Furthermore, the results for already tested hardware platforms are not provided by the benchmark creators. For AIBench, the component benchmarks and the datasets used are not mentioned in the Table III individually due to the vast number of domains targeted by this benchmark. The domains it targets in the component benchmark are Image classification, Image generation, Language translation, Image-to-Text, Image-to-Image, Speech recognition, Face embedding, 3D Face recognition, Object detection, Recommendation, Video prediction, Image compression, 3D object reconstruction, Text summarization, Spatial transformer, Learning to rank, and Neural architecture search. However, AIBench lacks in providing fixed rules for reproducing results. In comparison to MLPerf, there are no definite rules mentioned for data preprocessing nor which hyperparameters could be changed for each model individually. We consider tasks with image and video datasets as the most resource intensive therefore domains such as Image Classification and Object detection are sub-categorized as Resource intensive (RI). Reinforcement learning also uses image data and has additional complex tasks of control/action with some kind of update scheme therefore it is also added under the RI subcategory,

TABLE III
THE TABLE PROVIDES A SUMMARY OF THE SEVEN BENCHMARKS MENTIONED IN THIS PAPER.

Name	Dataset	Domain & Category	Metric
MLPerf	• ImageNeT • COCO • WMT Eng-Ger • 1TB Click Logs • Go	• Image classification (RI) • Object detection (RI) • Language Translation (RL) • NLP (RL) • Recommendation (RL) • Reinforcement learning (RI)	TTA
DAWN Bench	• ImageNet, Cifar10 • SQuAD	• Image classification (RI) • Question answering (RL)	TTA, Cost(in USD), Inference latency, Inference cost
Deep Bench	No real data used	• GEMM (SL) • Convolutional (SL) • Recurrent layers (SL) • All Reduce (SL)	Tera FLOPS, Total Time per operation (ms)
DLBS	Synthetic and real data (User provided dataset)	• Language translation (RL) • Image classification (RI)	Through-put, Batch time (ms)
TBD	• ImageNeT • IWSLT15 • LibriSpeech • Pascal VOC2007 • Downs. ImageNet • Atari	• Image classification (RI) • Machine Translation (RL) • Speech recognition (RL) • Object detection (RI) • Adversarial networks (RI) • Reinforcement learning (RI)	Through-put, GPU-Utilization, CPU-Utilization, F32-Utilization, Memory consumption
AIBench	• 17 different datasets	• 17 component benchmarks (E) • 14 micro benchmakrs (E)	TTA, TTE, Energy Consumption
ADA Bench	• Kaggle dataset • SMART dataset backblaze • Self generated • MovieLens	• Customer Service Management (RI) • Predictive Maintenance (RL) • Regression (RL) • Clustering (RL) • Classification (RI) • Recommendation (RL)	Throughput

VI. CRITICAL DISCUSSION TOWARDS AN IDEAL ML BENCHMARK

The benchmark suites mentioned in this paper lack a standard set of metrics. Even from the algorithmic point of view, a benchmark should offer multiple choices for a single domain. For example, all the mentioned benchmarks use classification accuracy as a metric for the Image classification domain. There are no options available to use Precision or Recall as a metric even with the fact that using accuracy only could be misleading. Besides, none of the mentioned benchmarks meet industrial needs as they do not allow user-specific datasets to be used (DLBS has that functionality but it targets only two domains). Domains like Image segmentation and Predictive maintenance are missing from the Domain level benchmarks. Furthermore, other than the MLPerf benchmark, no suite provides guidelines for having a fair comparison. These rules in MLPerf specify prime components such as the framework required for a particular domain (according to the reference implementation), loss function, and detailed information about the hyperparameter settings.

There is additionally a lack of support for testing cloud frameworks for ML. There are notable differences between different cloud providers. Platform such as Microsoft Azure [27] offer flexible compute options but have no built-in models whereas Google Cloud Platform (GCP) [28] offers auto ml tools with built-in models. The best cloud platform for ML is highly dependent on the application at hand. One has to carefully study the workflow used by these different providers and their data privacy regulations. Using cloud platforms would require data ingestion pipelines and additional processes which further increase the complexity. None of the benchmarks mentioned in this paper offer insights on any of these topics and neither do they provide any results for already tested cloud environments. Important metrics for comparing cloud platforms such as monetary cost, compute and storage performance are still missing from all the mentioned benchmarks (other than DAWNBench which has cost as a metric). Even prominent benchmarks such as MLPerf offer no guidelines for this cause. Even if one can transfer the reference implementation on a particular cloud framework, the datasets used, in some domains require high memory that adds to the overall cost. Furthermore, no metric available to compare the storage performances or cost of respective platforms discourages the idea of shifting the current benchmarks to cloud platforms.

We define an ideal benchmark that allows multiple domain specific metrics, e.g., in Image classification, one should be able to use ROC-AUC score instead of accuracy in TTA. It should fulfill the requirements mentioned in Section III. Moreover, it should also standardize rules through that other users could adapt their datasets for specific domains. These rules should also identify things that could be altered (e.g., hyperparameters, framework) to provide more flexibility but restrict changes that would damper the reproducibility aspect. Furthermore, these rules should be packed together with a reference implementation in a containerization format that is easily transferable to different machines without requiring fresh installations of every library required by the benchmark. Finally, it should also provide support for testing ever-growing cloud frameworks. This could be achieved by providing support for transferring containers of reference implementations on different cloud platforms with additional monetary metric.

VII. CONCLUSION

Rapid growth in ML has opened a vast number of options in hardware platforms for the user. In addition to local machines, various cloud computing platforms such as Amazon Web Services, Microsoft Azure, Google Cloud Platform, IBM Cloud, etc, are available for ML. These various cloud platforms offer the possibility of modeling storage and compute capacity that can be scaled according to the need of the users. The benchmarks mentioned in this paper other than DAWNBench do not target the cloud platforms directly.

In this paper, we have summarized seven prominent benchmarking suites that help in making an informed decision about which hardware or software is the best for a specific application. Some of the benchmarking suites are still in their development phases and in the future, they can accelerate further progress in their respective fields. Inferring from the last section, the different benchmark suites employ different metrics but there seems to be no agreement on a standardized set. None of the benchmarks provide any implementation for domains like predictive maintenance which is highly relevant for the manufacturing industry. With the addition of more domains, the inclusion of cost as a metric, improvement on documentation, and support for cloud platforms; the MLPerf and AIBench benchmark suites have the potential to become the go-to benchmarking suite for all ML applications.

ACKNOWLEDGEMENT

The contents of this publication are taken from the research project "(Q-AMeLiA) - Quality Assurance of Machine Learning Applications", funded by the Ministry of Science, Research and the Arts of the State of Baden-Württemberg (MWK BW) under reference number 32-7547.223-6/12/4, and supervised by Hochschule Furtwangen University (Prof. Dr. Christoph Reich, IDACUS). The responsibility for the content is with the authors.

REFERENCES

[1] S. Bouckaert, J. Gerwen, I. Moerman, S. C. Phillips, and J. Wilander, "Benchmarking computers and computer networks," *EU FIRE White Paper*, 2010.

[2] J. L. Hennessy and D. A. Patterson, *Computer architecture: a quantitative approach*. Elsevier, 2011.

[3] K. Ovtcharov, O. Ruwase, J.-Y. Kim, J. Fowers, K. Strauss, and E. S. Chung, "Accelerating deep convolutional neural networks using specialized hardware," *Microsoft Research Whitepaper*, vol. 2, no. 11, pp. 1–4, 2015.

[4] P. Mattson, C. Cheng, C. Coleman, G. Diamos, P. Micikevicius, D. Patterson, H. Tang, G.-Y. Wei, P. Bailis, V. Bittorf *et al.*, "Mlperf training benchmark," *arXiv preprint arXiv:1910.01500*, 2019.

[5] C. Coleman, D. Narayanan, D. Kang, T. Zhao, J. Zhang, L. Nardi, P. Bailis, K. Olukotun, C. Ré, and M. Zaharia, "Dawnbench: An end-to-end deep learning benchmark and competition," *Training*, vol. 100, no. 101, p. 102, 2017.

[6] B. Research, "DeepBench," https://github.com/baidu-research/DeepBench, 2018, [retrieved: March,2021].

[7] H. P. L. (HPL), "DLBS," https://github.com/HewlettPackard/dlcookbook-dlbs, 2018, [retrieved: March,2021].

[8] H. Zhu, M. Akrout, B. Zheng, A. Pelegris, A. Phanishayee, B. Schroeder, and G. Pekhimenko, "Tbd: Benchmarking and analyzing deep neural network training," *arXiv preprint arXiv:1803.06905*, 2018.

[9] W. Gao, F. Tang, L. Wang, J. Zhan, C. Lan, C. Luo, Y. Huang, C. Zheng, J. Dai, Z. Cao *et al.*, "Aibench: an industry standard internet service ai benchmark suite," *arXiv preprint arXiv:1908.08998*, 2019.

[10] T. Rabl, C. Brücke, P. Härtling, S. Stars, R. E. Palacios, H. Patel, S. Srivastava, C. Boden, J. Meiners, and S. Schelter, "Adabench-towards an industry standard benchmark for advanced analytics," in *Technology Conference on Performance Evaluation and Benchmarking*. Springer, 2019, pp. 47–63.

[11] K. M. Dixit, "The spec benchmarks," *Parallel computing*, vol. 17, no. 10-11, pp. 1195–1209, 1991.

[12] J. Gray, *Benchmark handbook: for database and transaction processing systems*. Morgan Kaufmann Publishers Inc., 1992.

[13] J. J. Dongarra, "Performance of various computers using standard linear equations software in a fortran environment," *ACM SIGARCH Computer Architecture News*, vol. 11, no. 5, pp. 22–27, 1983.

[14] W. Dai and D. Berleant, "Benchmarking contemporary deep learning hardware and frameworks: A survey of qualitative metrics," in *2019 IEEE First International Conference on Cognitive Machine Intelligence (CogMI)*. IEEE, 2019, pp. 148–155.

[15] O. Russakovsky, J. Deng, H. Su, J. Krause, S. Satheesh, S. Ma, Z. Huang, A. Karpathy, A. Khosla, M. Bernstein *et al.*, "Imagenet large scale visual recognition challenge," *International journal of computer vision*, vol. 115, no. 3, pp. 211–252, 2015.

[16] L. Beyer, O. J. Hénaff, A. Kolesnikov, X. Zhai, and A. v. d. Oord, "Are we done with imagenet?" *arXiv preprint arXiv:2006.07159*, 2020.

[17] C. Coleman, D. Kang, D. Narayanan, L. Nardi, T. Zhao, J. Zhang, P. Bailis, K. Olukotun, C. Ré, and M. Zaharia, "Analysis of dawnbench, a time-to-accuracy machine learning performance benchmark," *ACM SIGOPS Operating Systems Review*, vol. 53, no. 1, pp. 14–25, 2019.

[18] I. Goodfellow, Y. Bengio, and A. Courville, *Deep Learning*. MIT Press, 2016, http://www.deeplearningbook.org, [retrieved: March,2021].

[19] A. Krizhevsky, "Learning multiple layers of features from tiny images," *University of Toronto*, 05 2012.

[20] T. Lin, M. Maire, S. J. Belongie, L. D. Bourdev, R. B. Girshick, J. Hays, P. Perona, D. Ramanan, P. Doll'a r, and C. L. Zitnick, "Microsoft COCO: common objects in context," *CoRR*, vol. abs/1405.0312, 2014. [Online]. Available: http://arxiv.org/abs/1405.0312

[21] M. Everingham, L. Van Gool, C. K. I. Williams, J. Winn, and A. Zisserman, "The PASCAL Visual Object Classes Challenge 2007 (VOC2007) Results," http://www.pascal-network.org/challenges/VOC/voc2007/workshop/index.html, [retrieved: March,2021].

[22] O. Bojar, C. Buck, C. Federmann, B. Haddow, P. Koehn, J. Leveling, C. Monz, P. Pecina, M. Post, H. Saint-Amand, R. Soricut, L. Specia, and A. s. Tamchyna, "Findings of the 2014 workshop on statistical machine translation," in *Proceedings of the Ninth Workshop on Statistical Machine Translation*. Baltimore, Maryland, USA: Association for Computational Linguistics, June 2014, pp. 12–58. [Online]. Available: http://www.aclweb.org/anthology/W/W14/W14-3302

[23] C. A. Lab, "Criteo 1TB Click Logs dataset," https://ailab.criteo.com/criteo-1tb-click-logs-dataset/, [retrieved: March,2021].

[24] P. Rajpurkar, J. Zhang, K. Lopyrev, and P. Liang, "SQuAD: 100,000+ Questions for Machine Comprehension of Text," *arXiv e-prints*, p. arXiv:1606.05250, 2016.

[25] V. Panayotov, G. Chen, D. Povey, and S. Khudanpur, "Librispeech: an asr corpus based on public domain audio books," in *Acoustics, Speech and Signal Processing (ICASSP), 2015 IEEE International Conference on*. IEEE, 2015, pp. 5206–5210.

[26] BenchCouncil, "AIBench: A Datacenter AI Benchmark Suite, BenchCouncil," https://www.benchcouncil.org/AIBench/, 2019, [retrieved: March,2021].

[27] Microsoft, "Azure Machine Learning," https://azure.microsoft.com/de-de/services/machine-learning/, [retrieved: March,2021].

[28] Google, "Google Cloud Platform," https://cloud.google.com/products/ai, [retrieved: March,2021].

A Secure Access Control Architecture for Multi-Tenancy Cloud Environments

Ronald Beaubrun
Department of Computer Science and Software Engineering
Laval University
Quebec, Canada
e-mail: ronald.beaubrun@ift.ulaval.ca

Alejandro Quintero
Department of Computer and Software Engineering
Polytechnique Montreal
Montreal, Canada
e-mail: alejandro.quintero@polymtl.ca

Abstract— **In multi-tenancy cloud environments, physical resources are transparently shared by multiple Virtual Machines (VMs) belonging to multiple users. Implementing an efficient access control mechanism in such environments can prevent unauthorized access to the Cloud resources. In this paper, we propose an access control mechanism that provides scalable and secure access control to the Cloud in the context of multi-tenancy cloud environments. Such a mechanism will prevent malicious tenants from generating and sending unauthorized traffic to the Cloud network.**

Keywords-access control; cloud computing; hypervisor; multi-tenancy; security.

I. INTRODUCTION

Cloud computing is a flexible and cost-effective platform for providing business and consumer services over the Internet [1][8]. Such a platform is utilized by multiple customers who share computing resources, including CPU time, network bandwidth, data storage space, with other users, which refers to multi-tenancy [2]. By multi-tenancy, Clouds provide simultaneous, secure hosting of services for various customers utilizing the same infrastructure resources [3][9]. However, in multi-tenancy cloud environments, one customer can gain unauthorized access to the information of other customers. In this context, it is important to control the access of network entities to such information.

Access control is a security feature that controls how users and systems communicate and interact with other systems and resources. In general, there are three types of access control: physical access control, technical access control and administrative access control [5][11]. Physical access control refers to the implementation of security measures in a defined structure in order to prevent unauthorized access to sensitive materials. Examples of such control include: security guards, picture IDs, locked and dead-bolted steel doors, biometrics, closed-circuit surveillance cameras and motion or thermal alarm systems. Technical access control employs the technology as a basis for controlling the access to sensitive information throughout a physical structure and over a network. Examples of technical access control are: encryption, smart cards, network authentication, Access Control Lists (ACLs) and file integrity auditing software. Administrative access control defines the human factors of security. All levels of the personnel within an organization are involved in such control. Administrative access control also determines which users have access to which resources and information.

The above types of access control can be integrated into security architectures in order to preserve the integrity, confidentiality and availability of resources that are collocated in multi-tenancy Cloud environment. In this paper, we investigate the use of technical access control for proposing a secure access control mechanism in the context of multi-tenancy cloud environments. Such a mechanism will prevent malicious insiders from generating and sending unauthorized traffic to the cloud network.

The rest of the paper is organized as follows. Section II introduces the context and background related to access control in multi-tenancy cloud environments. Section III presents the main assumptions and principles of the proposed architecture. Section IV explains a use case scenario, whereas Section V gives some concluding remarks.

II. CONTEXT AND BACKGROUND

As illustrated in Figure 1, a multi-tenant Cloud service provider has three essential elements: the Cloud manager, the hypervisor and the Virtual Machines (VMs) [6]. The Cloud manager is a console of management provided for clients in order to manage their Cloud infrastructure, which means creating, shutting down, or starting the instances. The hypervisor, also called Virtual Machine Manager (VMM), allows multiple operating systems (guests or virtual machines) to run concurrently on a host server. Its main responsibility is to manage the application's operating systems (OSs) and their use of the system resources (e.g., CPU, memory and storage). Its role is to control the host processor and resources, and also to allocate what is needed to each operating system.

A VM is an isolated guest operating system installation within a normal host operating system. In this context, each client may have one or more VMs, as one physical server can host several VMs. In such an environment, one client can send unlimited amount of traffic to another client. Accordingly, a malicious agent can rent a VM on the same host where the target VM resides. This malicious agent can send unauthorized traffic to the target VM and violate the security of the target VM [10].

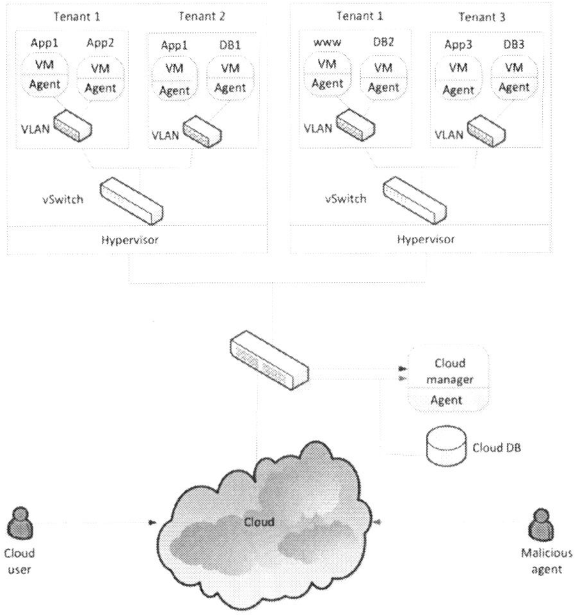

Figure 1. A model for a multi-tenant cloud service provider [6].

The unauthorized traffic may contain some script or malware which violates the confidentiality or the integrity of the target VM data. Sending such traffic to another VM makes it possible to perform other sorts of attacks. For instance, a malicious agent who owns a VM can perform VM Hopping over another user who is co-located at the same host. With VM hopping, an attacker has the control of one VM and tries to gain the control of another VM. VM hopping allows an attacker to move from one virtual server to the next one, or even to gain the root access to the physical hardware. VM hopping is a considerable threat because several VMs can run on the same host, which makes them the targets for the attacker. By performing this attack, a malicious user can violate the security and steal the data of other users who are located at the same server while compromising the hypervisor file system [4].

In addition, the malicious insider can perform Denial of Service (DoS) attacks. These kinds of attacks exhaust the resources of the Cloud network, such as bandwidth and computing power, by sending large amount of unauthorized traffic to other VMs.

III. EXISTING METHODS AND MODELS

In this section, we discuss the main existing methods and models for controlling access in the context of multi-tenancy cloud environments.

A. *Distributed access control*

The Distributed Access Control (DAC) architecture was proposed by Thomas et al. [12]. Such an architecture has three main components: the Cloud Service Provider (CSP), the Cloud Service Consumer (CSC) and the Identity Provider (IdP). The CSC requests the resources or services hosted by the CSPs. In this stage, the CSC should be first authenticated to ensure that unauthorized users do not access the services from the CSP. The main responsibility of the CSP is to host and to provide various services or resources to the CSCs. As a result, for avoiding illegal and unauthorized access by CSCs, proper authorization and authentication of CSCs are required.

Moreover, in DAC architecture, the IdP plays a great role since it generates identity tokens to the users. By using this identity token, a user can request the access to the cloud. Such a user may subscribe to services from multiple CSPs to meet the resource requirements. In this case, a federated identity management approach is required. The CSCs can use the identity tokens generated by the IdPs and these cloud users can exchange such tokens with various CSPs in the federation [12].

Analysis and results of DAC architecture reveal that using such an architecture is important in the domain of distributed applications or service computing. However, this model has some limitations. In particular, there is no effective mechanism which meets all access control requirements.

B. *Adaptive access algorithm*

Wang et al. [13] added trust management to the Role-Based Access Control (RBAC) in order to propose an adaptive access algorithm for cloud environments. This model is based on loyalty, i. e., a user is restricted only when its behavior contains malicious behavior. More specifically, the user request is first analyzed, and based on trust evaluation, the user becomes dynamically authorized. Here, user's trust is calculated according to user's behavior. In other words, the user access to the resource is dynamically based on calculation. As a result, by establishing dynamic mapping between roles and trust values, this model is able to determine the security level and control the user's access to the resources.

The trust-role-based-access control model claims that it can efficiently control user's malicious behavior. However, this model depends on the trust values, as the trust evaluation process needs to be improved in order to become widely used.

C. *Multi-tenancy access control model*

Multi-Tenancy Access Control Model (MTACM) is a security architecture which embeds the security duty separation principle in multi-tenancy cloud environments [14]. The main idea of MTACM is based on limiting the management privilege of CSP and letting the customers manage the security of their own business. In this model, the duty separation mechanism between cloud service provider and cloud customer is handled by a management module. However, the management module is not user-friendly for customers, as the cloud customer has to take care of the data security.

D. *Role-based multi-tenancy access control*

Role-Based Multi-Tenancy Access Control (RB-MTAC) applies identity management to determine user's identity and applicable roles [15]. Such a model combines two important concepts in access control under multi-tenancy access environment: identity management and role-based access control. In this context, Yang et al. [15] believe that this combination makes it easier to manage privileges that protect the security of application systems and data privacy. Providing a set of privileges and identity management schemes for corporations in cloud computing environment is the main contribution of this security model.

This scheme can be used to easily change employee privileges when a personnel member leaves an organization or when we want to grant employees more access without the need to modify all employee privileges one by one. However, RB-MTAC is not independent, and for implementing it in a cloud computing system, a directory service is needed.

E. *CloudPolice*

Popa et al. [7] proposed CloudPolice, a system that implements a hypervisor-based access control mechanism for multi-tenancy cloud environments. Since hypervisors are generally trusted, network-independent, close to VMs and fully software programmable, CloudPolice seems to be effective to prevent denial of service (DoS) attacks from malicious agents who send unauthorized traffic to their targets. As a result, CloudPolice acts as stateful firewalls and creates a state for each flow.

However, there are several major concerns for the feasibility of CloudPolice. The first concern is the ability for the hypervisor to act on per flow state, as the hypervisor should be ready to act on every single flow. The second concern is the ability to install new state with low enough latencies for new traffic flows, as we should make sure that the hypervisor is able to create a state for each new incoming flow very fast. As a result, the hypervisor should be able to create states for all new flows without latency (or at least with acceptable latency) and also act on the states that already exist in the buffer. Also, CloudPolice imposes overheads in the system, as the destination hypervisor receives all the traffic and decides to pass or drop the traffic based on the security attributes of the target virtual machines.

IV. THE PROPOSED ARCHITECTURE

This section defines the main assumptions, as well as the design and principles of the proposed architecture.

A. *Main assumptions*

The proposed architecture deals with the concept of Inter-VM traffic, which is the transmission of any data packet to and from one virtual machine. In other words, when the hypervisor encounters inter-VM traffic, the traffic does not pass through the physical switch or router, as the virtual switch that is located at the hypervisor forwards the packet to the destination VM. At this point, the following assumptions need to be done:

- The virtual machines and physical servers are co-located at the same cloud provider. If the entire system is not part of the Cloud, then for sending traffic to another Cloud, the traffic should pass through a real router or firewall. In this case, the policies that are implemented in the firewall should be enforced.
- Each physical server has only one hypervisor. In this case, the security attributes and access control lists of all virtual machines that belong to a physical server are located at one hypervisor. If we have multiple hypervisors on a physical server, we should apply an extra process for realizing which hypervisor contains the access control lists of certain virtual machines.
- Each physical server is hosting at least one tenant, and each tenant has at least one virtual machine. Since each virtual machine should be registered as a tenant, if a tenant is registered in the Cloud, a virtual machine should be assigned to that tenant.
- All access control lists are defined and stored in the hypervisor.
- In its startup process, a hypervisor sends an update message to the other hypervisors that are located at the same Cloud. This update message contains the IP address and the ID of virtual machines that are located at that hypervisor.

B. *Architecture principles*

The principles of the proposed architecture are based on control packets, which is the core element for verifying security permissions of virtual machines in multi-tenancy Cloud environments. In this section, we explain the elements of the proposed access control architecture, which is illustrated in Figure 2.

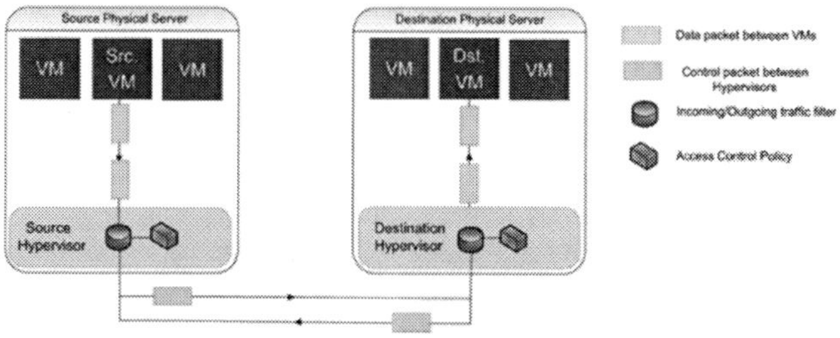

Figure 2. Principles of the proposed architecture.

- Source (Src.) VM is a virtual machine that is installed on the source hypervisor, as the latter is located at the physical source server. The source VM is then sending traffic packets to a virtual machine in the same Cloud called Dst. VM.
- Destination (Dst.) VM is installed at the destination hypervisor, and this hypervisor is located at the destination physical server.

- A data packet is a packet that the source VM wants to send to the destination VM.
- A control packet is a special packet that is generated by the source hypervisor. Its content represents the specifications of the source and destination VMs.
- Incoming/outgoing traffic filter is a lightweight IDS that is integrated in the hypervisor. It compares the control packet with the access control lists of destination VM.
- An access control list is a set of security permission that defines the level of security of each virtual machine.

C. *Architecture design*

The main goal of the proposed architecture is to block and drop undesired packets as close as possible of the source hypervisor. As illustrated in Figure 2, when the source VM sends traffic to the destination VM, such traffic has to pass through the source hypervisor. As soon as a data packet reaches the hypervisor, it generates a control packet which consists of the necessary information for access control checking, such as the source IP address, the destination IP address, the port numbers, as well as the protocol type. Such a control packet has to be sent to the destination hypervisor which checks its content and decides whether the traffic can be delivered to the destination hypervisor. If the source VM is permitted to send the so-called traffic to the destination VM, the destination hypervisor adds a pass or drop value to the control packet payload, and sends it back to the source hypervisor. According to this value, the source hypervisor threats the awaiting traffic.

As illustrated in Figure 3, the process starts when a VM initiates to send some traffic to another VM. As soon as such traffic is received by the source hypervisor, it checks the packet and looks for the destination address that is located at the inserted IP packet header. If the destination address belongs to a virtual machine in the same cloud, we will have two possibilities. The first case considers that the destination address is located at the same physical server. In this case, the architecture checks the access control policy of the destination VM, and can decide whether to pass or drop the traffic. The second case occurs when the destination address is located at a different physical server. In this case, the source hypervisor generates and sends the control packet to the destination hypervisor. Then, it waits for the response control packet.

Beside such possibilities, there may be an exception, when the destination address does not belong to any VM in this cloud, which means that the source and destination addresses belong to two devices that are not co-located at the same Cloud. In this case, the architecture only has to pass the traffic to the default gateway of the source hypervisor (router, switch or firewall).

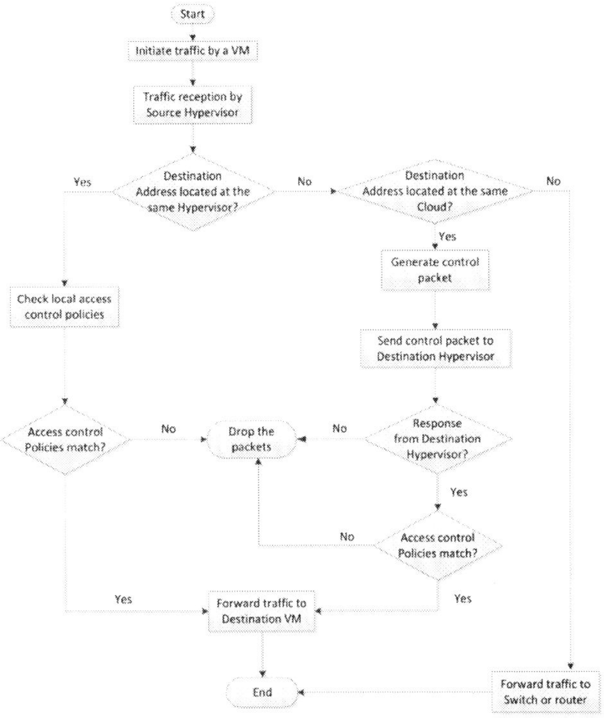

Figure 3. General mechanism flowchart.

The main part of the mechanism starts if the destination address belongs to a VM that is located at a destination hypervisor. In this case, the whole traffic should wait until the source hypervisor generates and sends a control packet to the destination hypervisor. Hence, the decision will be made based on the response control packet. Figure 4 shows the main tasks of the destination hypervisor when it receives the control packet from the source hypervisor. More precisely, the destination hypervisor selects one of the following actions:

- Insert a pass value to the control packet if the access control policy of the destination VM matches, and accept the traffic from the source VM.
- Insert a drop value to the control packet if the access control policy of the destination VM does not match, as the source VM is not authorized to send the traffic to the destination VM.
- Insert a null value to the control packet if the destination address is not found in the destination hypervisor. This may happen if the control packet is sent to the hypervisor by mistake, or if the VM destination is migrated to another hypervisor, whereas the source hypervisor is not informed about such migration.

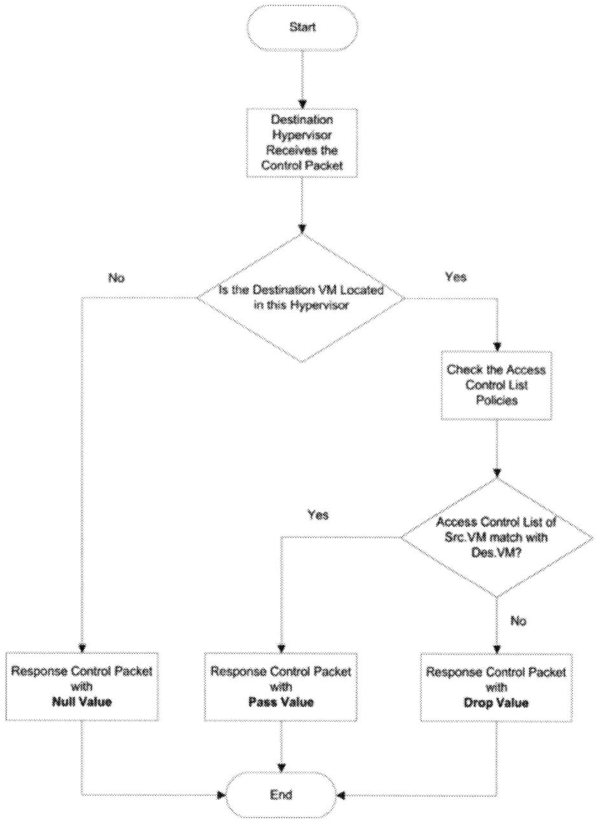

Figure 4. Destination hypervisor's tasks after control packet reception.

After inserting the proper value to the control packet, the destination hypervisor returns the edited control packet to the source hypervisor. The response control packet contains the decision and the action to be taken for the traffic. In the case of a drop value, the source hypervisor drops the traffic right away, as such traffic will not even exit the hypervisor, which means no wasted and unnecessary traffic in the network. Consequently, the network bandwidth does not suffer from extra and unwanted traffic. Finally, the pass value indicates that the access control policy matches between the source and destination, whereas the source VM and the traffic will pass throughout the destination hypervisor.

V. A USE CASE SCENARIO

In this section, we analyze a use case scenario which enables to tackle the problem of sending unauthorized traffic to a VM in the context of multi-tenancy Cloud environments. This scenario is illustrated in Figure 5, where a public Cloud is connected to the Internet, using a router and three physical servers that are connected to a layer-2 switch. In this scenario, the function of the router is to route the internal traffic of the Cloud to the Internet. Apparently, the router serves as a controller, enabling the networked devices to talk to each other efficiently.

In this scenario, there are 3 physical servers, as well as 10 virtual machines. These virtual machines belong to 4 tenants. The multi-tenancy topology of this Cloud is as follows:

- Server 1: Tenant 1 (VM1, VM2) and Tenant 2 (VM3)
- Server 2: Tenant 1 (VM4, VM5) and Tenant 3 (VM6, VM7)
- Server 3: Tenant 4 (VM8) and Tenant 3 (VM9, VM10)

It is important to mention that the process of controlling the access is executed in the hypervisors. In this context, the scenario has two phases: the first phase consists of generating control packets, whereas in the second phase, the destination hypervisor investigates the information and decides about the destiny of the packet. More specifically, in phase one of the scenario, the VM Source sends a traffic flow to the hypervisor source, as illustrated in stage 1 of Figure 6. Then, the source hypervisor generates a control packet. The content of this control packet is based on the traffic to be sent from source VM3 to destination VM8.

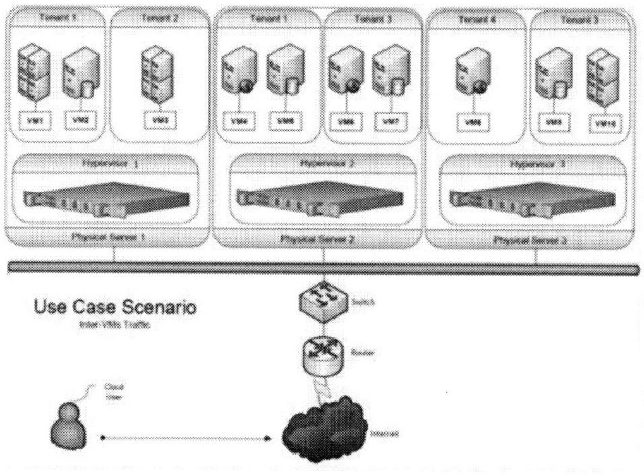

Figure 5. A use case scenario for multi-tenancy cloud access control.

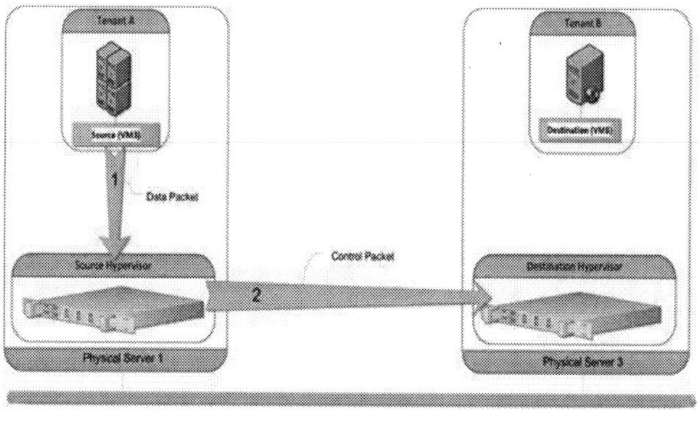

Figure 6. Illustration of phase one of the scenario.

As illustrated in stage 2 of Figure 6, the source hypervisor sends the control packet to the destination hypervisor in order to check the access control policy of the VM destination.

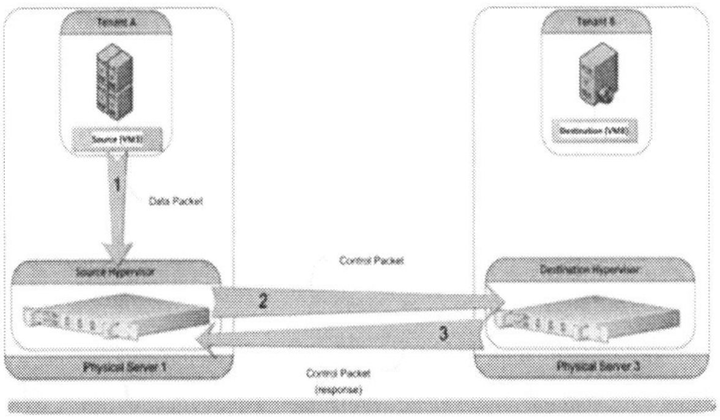

Figure 7. Illustration of phase two of the scenario.

In phase two, the control packet arrives at the destination hypervisor which checks the access control lists (ACLs) to verify if VM3 is authorized to send traffic to VM8. If the ACLs related to VM8 match, the destination hypervisor sends back a pass value within the control packet (called response control packet) to the source hypervisor, as illustrated in stage 3 of Figure 7. The response control packet enables the hypervisor source to decide what to do with the traffic that is waiting in the source hypervisor. Hence, if the security attributes of VM8 do not match the data packet, then the destination hypervisor sends a drop signal to the source hypervisor.

VI. Conclusion

The access control architecture proposed in this paper for multi-tenancy Cloud environments satisfies a number of the requirements, such as scalability and security. This architecture is scalable in the sense that, if the number of VMs grows, we only need to implement this architecture in the hypervisor of each physical server without any extra changes in the system. Besides that, the architecture enables to maintain the security of information in the Cloud system by controlling the traffic sent from one hypervisor to another hypervisor and by enforcing the security policies in the hypervisor. Using such an architecture leads to better performance by avoiding unnecessary traffic and dedicating the Cloud resources to necessary traffic. Future works will focus on implementing a prototype of the proposed architecture on a real Cloud environment.

References

[1] K. Hashizume, D. G. Rosado, E. Fernández-Medina, and E. B. Fernandez, "An analysis of security issues for cloud computing," Journal of Internet Services and Applications 4:5, vol. 4, 2013, pp. 5-18.

[2] Z. Minqi, Z. Rong, X. Wei, Q. Weining, and Z. Aoying, "Security and Privacy in Cloud Computing: A Survey," in 6th International Conference Semantics Knowledge and Grid (SKG), , Beijing, 2010, pp. 105-112.

[3] C. J. Guo, W. Sun, Y. Huang, Z. H. Wang, and B. Gao, "A framework for native multitenancy application development and management," in 9th International Conference on E-Commerce Technology/4th International Conference on Enterprise Computing, Ecommerce and E-Services, Tokyo, 2007, pp. 551-558.

[4] A. Jasti, P. Shah, R. Nagaraj, and R. Pendse, "Security in Multi-Tenancy Cloud," in International Carnahan Conference on Security Technology (ICCST), , San Jose, CA, 2010, pp. 35-41.

[5] S. Harris, CISSP All-in-One Exam Guide, Sixth ed. New York: McGraw-Hill, 2013.

[6] K. Benzidane, S. Khoudali, and A. Sekkaki, "Autonomous Agent-based Inspection for inter-VM Traffic in a Cloud Environment," in 7th International Conference for Internet Technology and Secured Transactions (ICITST-2012), London, 2012, pp. 656-661.

[7] L. Popa, M. Yu, S. Y. Ko, S. Ratnasamy, and I. Stoica, "CloudPolice: Taking Access Control out of the Network," in ACM Workshop on Hot Topics in Networks. HotNets, Monterey, CA, USA, 2010, pp. 1-6.

[8] M. Auxilia and K. Raja, "Dynamic Access Control Model for Cloud Computing," Sixth International Conference on Advanced Computing (ICoAC), pp. 47-56, 2014.

[9] G. Kappes, A. Hatzieleftheriou, and S. V. Anastasiadis., "Multitenant Access Control for Cloud-Aware Distributed Filesystems," IEEE Transactions on Dependable and Secure Computing, Vol. 16, No. 6, pp. 1070-1085, 2019.

[10] S. J. De and S. Ruj, "Efficient Decentralized Attribute Based Access Control for Mobile Clouds," IEEE Transactions on Cloud Computing, Vol. 8, No. 1, pp. 124-137, 2020.

[11] K. Albulayhi, A. Abuhussein, F. Alsubaei, and F.T. Sheldon, "Fine-Grained Access Control in the Era of Cloud Computing: An Analytical Review," 10th Annual Computing and Communication Workshop and Conference (CCWC), pp. 748 – 755, 2020.

[12] M. V. Thomas and K. C. Sekaran, "An Access Control Model for Cloud Computing Environments," in 2nd International Conference on Advanced Computing, Networking and Security (ADCONS), Mangalore, pp. 226-231, 2013.

[13] W. Wenhui, H. Jing, S. Meina, and W. Xiaohui, "The design of a trust and role based access control model in cloud computing," in 6th International Conference on Pervasive Computing and Applications (ICPCA), Port Elizabeth, pp. 330-334, 2011.

[14] X.-Y. Li, Y. Shi, Y. Guo, and W. Ma, "Multi-Tenancy Based Access Control in Cloud," in International Conference on Computational Intelligence and Software Engineering (CiSE), Wuhan, pp. 1-4, 2010.

[15] S.-J. Yang, P.-C. Lai, and J. Lin, "Design Role-Based Multi-tenancy Access Control Scheme for Cloud Services," in International Symposium on Biometrics and Security Technologies (ISBAST), Chengdu, pp. 273-279, 2013.

Take Me to the Clouds Above: Bridging On Site HPC with Clouds for Capacity Workloads

Jay Lofstead
Sandia National Laboratories
Albuquerque, NM, USA
email: gflofst@sandia.gov

Dmitry Duplyakin
School of Computing, University of Utah
Salt Lake City, UT, USA
email: dmdu@cs.utah.edu

***Abstract*—Sites with limited compute cluster capacity aimed at supporting large-scale applications of scientific and parallel computing must deal with the additional demand for small-scale jobs—in many cases, single-node and coming in large volumes—that help further develop the capabilities of large-scale applications as well as run simple data analysis tasks. Many of these analysis tasks and other small-scale jobs are run on High Performance Computing (HPC) systems because they offer familiar environments, making future scaling convenient, or because the proximity to the input or output data sets is important. When these small-scale jobs explode in count and create significant competition for resources, ensuring that the most effective use of the cluster resources is achieved requires either non-trivial scheduler tuning for better management of job mixes or adoption of entirely different models for management of computing environments. We claim that a hybrid "on-site HPC + cloud" model can offer the best of both worlds. Thus, small jobs should target cloud resources in cases where they can be offloaded to clouds without significant penalties on performance, and, at the same time, large-scale application runs can better utilize HPC clusters, achieving lower wait times and increasing job throughput. This is not without challenges.**

***Index Terms*—HPC, Cloud, cloud bursting, job scheduling**

I. Introduction

Organizations with large-scale computing needs constantly have to balance two different workloads on their computing infrastructures. Some target workloads include *large-scale, scale-up* jobs that often use extra hardware. For exmaple, (Graphic Processing Units) GPUs offer extreme parallel processing at lower power usage, but with limitations on accessing resources outside the GPU package or potentially even other processes on the GPU. Field Programmable Gate Arrays, FPGAs, offer a way to program hardware enabling very low power processing with a highly customized processing structure. These kinds of speciality tools are becoming more common as ways to achieve more compute efficiency at large scale. At the same time, workloads with *small-scale* jobs need to co-exist on these systems with large-scale jobs. These workloads include much smaller jobs for development, analysis, and initial exploration that need tiny fractions of the available resources and may not be optimized to take advantage of the specialized hardware. Supporting both types of workloads and achieving good balance between them are important components of computing missions within many organizations, in academic, research, and commercial sectors.

For example, Sandia National Laboratories (Sandia) has workloads that match these patterns. At Sandia, we field a large machine (Trinity [1]) in cooperation with Los Alamos National Lab as well as smaller but still decently sized machines (e.g., Astra [2]) on our own. In spite of this compute capability, Sandia still fields numerous additional clusters to handle capacity needs. The intent is for the capacity machines to serve for development and small scale runs prompting scheduler priorities to focus on first fit rather than job age or size related priorities. Part of the challenge for Sandia is the presence of export controlled or classified computing jobs prompting on site computing resources expansion. Using a public, shared resource may not be possible due to the security restrictions. Some of the concerns with running specific workloads related to export control or sensitive or classified data or processing have special requirements of the cloud platform and the connection with it. Certification [3] can allow workloads and data for some workloads while higher consequence and more sensitive information still cannot use these infrastructures.

Even with this generous compute capacity on site, Sandia still has computing demands that could best be served in a cloud environment based on tool requirements or data locality, such as work on a cloud hosted, shared data set. Integrating these systems, particularly considering the security concerns, is problematic.

Smaller HPC systems, such as, for instances, university clusters and machines at smaller research laboratories, have similar usage demands but not as much computing capacity available. Unlike Sandia, many of these systems do not have strong security requirements, which allows their users to freely leverage public cloud resources as overflow capacity. However, even in the organizations where cloud transition is acceptable and supported by the internal cloud teams, not all users migrate their smaller jobs to the cloud resources. Such migration has much potential for on-site resources to be better serving the workloads that depend on their availability, yet this potential is primarily unrealized within the organization.

One hurdle to integrating multiple platforms is the lack of effective cross platform schedulers and job build and deployment resources. During the grid era, numerous efforts attempted to make a single front-end for various grid back-end systems [4]. They all suffered from complexity of different back-end system features and architectures, among other limitations.

In this context, the question of tools to address this from a policy and technology infrastructure basis need to be explored to inform effectively addressing workload balancing.

The rest of this paper is structured as follows. First, in Section II, we discuss the state of the art for job schedulers in HPC and cloud computing as well as the challenges that arise in integration of resources from different sources. Next, in Section III, we describe the cloud-related challenges and opportunities as they have been explored in various hybrid and multi-cloud studies. Next, Section IV presents a survey of related work. A discussion of recommendations on how to approach solving the hybrid bursting problem is discussed in Section V. Finally, Section VI offers takeaway requirements and challenges we need to address as a community to achieve seamless on site HPC and public cloud resources, whether the cloud has high security instances or not.

II. Job Scheduling

Task scheduling system generally fall into one of three categories with some newer systems attempting to bridge either the categories, platforms supported, or both.

A. *Scale Up Task Scheduling*

The predominant scheduler in use in HPC centers today is Slurm [5]. As an open source tool with strong community support, it has grown to handle most HPC compute management needs. In particular, it has recently been enhanced to offer support for multi-resource scheduling [6]. This enables heterogeneous node types to be effectively scheduled ensuring that jobs that require special hardware will only run on nodes that can support them while ensuring that jobs that do not need that special hardware do not overly delay the special jobs.

While Slurm is certainly not the only scheduler available, it is dominant at the USA's Federally Funded Research and Development Centers as it reduces costs and better supports building affordable infrastructure for the private sector to use. Other schedulers are discussed briefly in the related work in Section IV.

A next generation HPC scheduler, Flux [7] offers these features and is intending to extend into supporting integrated cloud infrastructures. However, Flux is just starting to explore how to incorporate cloud resources and has only scratched the surface of the vast complexities involved. It will take considerable time and effort for Flux to successfully integrate a single cloud platform. In the meantime, recommendations and policy changes that can be implemented quickly will offer relief.

HPC oriented schedulers focus on a single task or small number of tasks per job with each task potentially using 10000 nodes or more for each task. The priority is to gather sufficient resources according to the scheduler policy settings to successfully run each queued job at the right time. In these cases, task scheduling throughput in the 100s of jobs/tasks per second is sufficient to address the workload needs.

B. *Scale Out Task Scheduling*

At the other extreme are scale out workloads. These tend into two categories. First are the many data analytics tasks or other job types that add additional compute to reduce compute time. They use independent processing and can just divide the workload into more parts to achieve faster throughput. Genomics processing is one example with a massive data set that can be divided into many independent pieces for exploring matching against another genetic sequence. These tasks tend to be smaller, maybe 10s of nodes at most, and can be restarted independently if one should fail without affecting the other tasks. The other category is rapidly running tasks that collectively perform a more complex operation. If a task runs for 1 second or less, the scheduler must be able to schedule many thousands per second across a large machine to keep the scheduler from being the throughput bottleneck. Some modern software engineering architectures, such as function-as-a-service [8], embrace this kind of short task execution model as a central feature.

The need to handle scheduling a large number of short running tasks prompted the creation of Sparrow [9] and similar systems. This shift from the traditional very large single task with a long run time demanded these new tools to better handle resource use.

With large scale task oriented systems, task scheduling throughput more on the order of 10000s is required to ensure the compute is the bottleneck rather than the scheduler. Different job schedulers oriented for this environment, such as for Spark [10], offer better throughput using different base assumptions. For example, a single tasks can be scheduled either on a single node or a single core making resource selection a far easier task. Considerations about interference effects from interconnect network traffic are not important. Other interference effects, such as those from cache sharing, are typically not a top priority. Mesos [11] with systems like Aurora [12] and Yarn [13] offer examples of high throughput task oriented schedulers.

Other systems like Omega [14] were built in frustration of the need to support heterogeneous clusters that evolved as new hardware was added over time with broken and obsolete hardware decommissioned. The priority for a system like this is to support a wide variety of hardware features and enable a reasonably efficient mapping from job requirements onto the available hardware balancing needs against availability.

C. *Container Orchestration*

The alternative approach for job scheduling has shifted more to container management rather than task management. Systems like Kubernetes [15] and Docker Swarm [16] offer increasingly rich and complex environments for deploying long-lived services that can dynamically scale on demand. This is a fundamentally different kind of workload making it a poor match for either scale out or scale up workloads without rethinking their architectures.

D. Discussion

The kinds of workloads each of these system classes addresses is different and difficult to address with a single scheduler and resource management system. This has led to the fragmentation of platform development efforts, where each platform is essentially treated as an independent direction for research and development and optimized to best address its own, particular subset of the workloads.

The real challenge being faced by large scale compute centers today is that the various tools used in each of these different environments are starting to be demanded within others. For example, machine learning tools are now being incorporated into scientific simulations. For example, in climate simulations [17], [18], machine learning models are substituting for parts of the model that may have too many parameters or the physics is not fully understood. Using models generated from observational data, reasonable estimates of these effects improve the simulation model quality overall.

Other examples of cross platform tool usage include data analytics tools for use on simulation generated data sets. Being able to run the analytics tools with the simulation would accelerate insight discovery by shortening the exploration time. How to best handle these hybrid workloads further complicates the scheduling picture.

III. Cloud Challenges and Opportunities

Public cloud systems are essentially walled gardens offering data storage, compute capacity, and often, many tools and services that make application development fast and easy. This is quite attractive for many different disciplines enabling less costly tech company startup costs (i.e., outsource all of the compute infrastructure needed to an on-demand cloud service eliminating the need for hardware purchases for peak usage times and hiring system administrators). Fueling innovation is not the only advantage. Other institutions that need a relatively large amount of computing power for a short period of time find cloud services a cost effective approach to meeting their computing needs.

In spite of the advantages offered, trying to combine a single cloud environment with either a second cloud or another platform is far from an easy or inexpensive endeavour.

A. Performance

A large number of studies reported performance limitations and downsides of cloud computing environments [19]–[21]. These studies pointed out the lack of low-latency networks, high virtualization overheads, significant performance variability due to resource sharing, among other concerns. However, one common fact about these studies is that it has been nearly a decade since they have been published and, therefore, the results they include essentially relate to the clouds of previous generations. On the contrary, the offerings from today's clouds provide access to resources with impressive processor performance, increased memory sizes, and highly optimized networks in isolation from other user's traffic. Additionally, a recent comprehensive study [22] indicates that the performance gap between HPC and clouds is essentially closed, at least at small and moderate scales. In fact, it is shown that a cloud system offers higher bandwidth and lower latency than a production HPC system, deployed as recently as several years ago.

B. Data Movement

One of the most serious concerns with cloud-based processing is the data movement. Cloud systems, such as Amazon Web Services, offer free data ingress as an enticement for moving a data set onto the service and to use their compute resources. However, while data movement onto the platform is free, moving data out frequently incurs a charge. Also, data storage on the platform usually involves charges as well. With limited ingress bandwidth, storing large datasets for repeated processing becomes the only reasonable option forcing recurring costs. A related challenge may be the security of data migraion between platforms [23].

C. Spot Pricing

In many cases, cloud pricing is not fixed, but varies dynamically based on supply and demand. In these cases, trying to control compute job costs by migrating between clouds or moving from an HPC resource to a cloud is further complicated. Effectively managing these costs variances has led to management systems [24]. It is a far from simple task to achieve the lowest costs compute, particularly when data movement delays and costs are incorporated.

D. Job Requirements

The way applications are packaged for use on an HPC resource compared to each different cloud is different. In some cases, it is a container. In others, it is virtual machines. Others still require that you build your application in the cloud environment and it is stored using an internal format, typically something similar to a virtual machine. With an HPC job that uses Slurm or any of the other HPC-oriented schedulers, the applications and job scripts have been written and optimized for a particular platform with specific dynamic library versions available and access to particular storage systems with specific interfaces. For example, the S3 interface on AWS has a completely different interface than the typical POSIX API of an HPC scratch space or one of the database (SQL or NoSQL both) systems. Key-value stores have yet another interface, although it is most similar to S3. This variety of tools required for processing makes deploying an application automatically from and HPC to cloud or vice versa a difficult proposition.

E. Discussion

While the cloud environment is best (cheapest) when it can be used with small, transient data on a single cloud data center, the above research demonstrates the potential benefits and deep challenges with effectively combining one cloud data center with some other compute resource, be it another cloud or an onsite HPC or cloud platform. The challenges are not insurmountable, but are difficult.

The different deployment and job scheduling interfaces are serious challenges that are not a simple matter of money. Instead they require significant research and development effort to construct a reasonable approach that considers many of the challenges identified above and the others not listed here.

In spite of these challenges and costs involved, cloud can also be a better option to manage on site inter-group conflicts. For example, at the 2017 University of California, Santa Cruz CROSS Symposium [25], the genomics institute talked about why they used AWS for their workloads even though they had sufficient infrastructure on site to handle their workloads. The challenge came down to having a third party arbiter for who should pay for what and how much they use. For example, if a researcher is using "paid for" on campus compute, they may demand to keep 10 PiB of data because it is all precious. That same researcher, when presented with a US$20,000 bill for storing that data, they may suddenly decide that more than 90% of it was not that critical after all. Further, by using the third party arbiter, deciding who gets to use the compute and when is more a matter of just allocating budget rather than arguments over whose turn it is to use the machines. Even though the costs can be significantly higher than on site resources, having the direct costs and third party arbiter proved to be a significant advantage for managing multiple research groups using a shared resource.

IV. Related Work

Two commercial job schedulers for HPC workloads include the Cray scheduler (ALPS) [26] and IBM Cobalt Scheduler [27]. Both of these systems offer full features and excellent performance optimized for their proprietary platform environment, but are limited to the vendor platforms. With the strong emphasis on open source for HPC through efforts like OpenHPC [28], these systems offer a difficult value proposition. Users can get the same tools across a variety of platforms, but have to switch their job scripts and other management infrastructure for every user if adopting one of the proprietary platforms.

The literature that discusses HPC systems at national laboratories [29]–[31] provides rich information about HPC usage trends, resource utilization metrics, evolution of supercomputers over time, among many other user- and system-centered topics. Most of the existing studies on HPC environments—both historic and also recent—pay little attention to cloud computing and its benefits, considering integration with clouds to be secondary or optional in nature. With the shifting workload demands, revisiting these investigations is an important priority.

Among the counterexamples, a study of computing resources at the Texas Advanced Computing Center (TACC) [32] stands out as it describes a considerable number of cloud-style jobs being processed as a result of integration of TACC facilities with Jetstream [33], a cloud computing facility sponsored and managed by the USA's National Science Foundation (NSF).

Chameleon Cloud [34] offers a bare-metal-as-a-service cloud option. While this is an NSF supported effort focused on supporting both research and education, the resources are not as extreme as leadership computing facilities. Instead, the focus is on supporting smaller scale efforts with a strong tie to educational environments rather than production-style workloads.

CloudLab [35] and other cloud testbeds offer a different take on the cloud environment by incorporating new hardware and software to test out how to use these new tools in a cloud environment. These systems, while looking at experimental system design, do not have the strong ties to a production HPC environment nor the capacity to handle offload for a heavy workload.

With traditional HPC requiring more specialized system administration capabilities and more expert friendly compute management interfaces, the cloud oriented environment enables running scale out workloads or even scale up workloads with friendlier tools. Academic institutions trying to address their entire user base focus on the majority users with a cloud-friendly configuration that can also support, albiet without fully optimized configurations, scale up computing workloads to some degree. This has been discussed in good detail by Hwang, et al. [36].

The final part of the related work concerns cloud bursting. These systems look at how to use a cloud resource as "overflow" for an onsite or just another large scale compute resource. Work on these bursting approaches [19], [37], [38] show the challenges and potential for making these systems work. Microsoft, with the Azure platform, offer this as a fundamental part of their cloud strategy. They encourage users to install an Azure instance at their premises and to use Microsoft's private cloud instances as bursting capacity. This enables customers to right size their on site compute resources to control costs while not hitting limits for transient peak workloads. Achieving this kind of balance for HPC and Cloud would offer an excellent balance by deploying jobs that do not need the HPC platform characteristics onto the associated cloud when there is demand for the HPC platform specific characteristics by jobs. However, these capabilities still do not exist.

V. Recommendations

As with most things in life, you get what you measure and what you reward. In this case, using incentives can change behavior prompting users to move workload most compatible with cloud infrastructures off the on-site HPC resources. Rewarding "good behavior" while monitoring systems to detect "bad beahvior", these goals can be achieved quickly.

We were unable to find any publications about these kinds of management strategies prompting our work to formalize the understanding of the problem space and start investigating and measuring solution effectiveness. This paper is the first step in that process.

A. Long Term

Long term, using a scheduler like Flux, once it has fully incorporated cloud capabilities, will be the "correct" choice for managing multi-platform resources with varying workload characteristics. By "correct", we mean that it will offer a general, simple, least cost way to bridge between the platforms with low user involvement. Other approaches will likely still be better for specific use cases. In the mean time, some simpler approaches can be used to encourage users to reconsider which platform they run their workloads on.

Also long term, adopting a Kubernetes-like environment with virtual machines and containers, deploying different workloads may be easier at a performance and complexity cost. Versioning these artifacts makes reproducibility and replicability of computational science easier as a side effect and worth considering for simply that reason. Further discussion about this topic is beyond the scope of this paper.

B. Short Term

Short term approaches focus on the encouragement via measurement and reward approaches. Below are a selection of ideas to explore in this space.

First, judicially use time-based priority based on job size and resource requirement. For tiny jobs, impose something like a 1 year age penalty for scheduling priority. For large jobs, give a bonus. Then the scheduler can automatically adjust which jobs get run. While this seems simplistic, it can offer a basic metric to shift the workload balance. Gaming the system by allocating more resources than needed is likely prompting other approaches in combination (see below).

Second, adjust allocations and priority based on how the compute resources are used. For example, if nodes have GPUs, ensuring that jobs significantly use the GPUs, can improve effective usage. In this case, monitoring system characteristics, such as power and heat on different system components, can yield a better measure of what kind of work a particular job actually performs. This can offer bonuses or penalties for future compute use based on the past job characteristics. This is not a perfect measure since a user could incorporate a GPU benchmark running in the background while their simple CPU-only workload runs, the additional effort to incorporate such cheating is not worth the effort. With policy that could ban users for such behavior and user support to use alternative resources, such as cloud systems, the chances are reduced considerably. For special cases, a user could apply for an exemption for a special project enabling exceptional cases while automating a strong policy. In combination with the time priority, the instances of cheating can be greatly curtailed.

Third, consider offering HPC allocation bonuses based on cloud usage. If a user makes an effort to run their smaller jobs on the cloud, rewarding them with additional large run compute allocations can make achieving their scientific goals easier and faster. Once the learning curve of using the cloud is mastered, the user becomes bi-lingual and can deploy on whatever platform makes the most sense. This is not an easy goal to achieve, but possible with minimal system interventions and offering training and user support that is likely currently supported within the organization.

Overall, any attempt to encourage users to take advantage of a second platform needs to consider the added complexity for the user. What benefit (or avoided penalty) is the user gaining by spending the distraction time to learn how to use a new platform? Also, these need to consider that the approach may work too well causing a mass migration to the cloud leaving an expensive HPC resource underused. While this latter case is less likely, it is a consideration if the penalties are too harsh.

These are but three approaches under evaluation. Others are certainly possible and left as future work.

VI. Conclusions

Throughout the paper, we have presented a series of requirements and challenges with integrating cloud with on site HPC. A highlight of these requirements and challenges are presented below.

For requirements, first, in all cases, training will be critical to help users understand how to use a new computing platform with different interfaces and software packing requirements. Second, proper incentives can help encourage users that are in the best interest of the overall user community. Third, considering the full cost of moving compute from one platform to another needs to be considered. Data movement in particular can incur long delays and significant costs.

For challenges, first, offering strong enough incentives that users are willing to consider using a very different platform without them moving all of their use is a delicate balance. Too little and the on site HPC still is dominated by jobs that could be offloaded. Too harsh and users will just use the cloud for everything even though the on site HPC may sit mostly idle. Second, offering a seamless interface that deploys on either platform is the ideal goal. However, the numerous challenges related to application deployment, data movement, and job submission differences have proven challenging for scientific computing system interfaces. Significant investment in these areas is required for a usable system. Third, managing costs on spot priced clouds makes deploying jobs an activity potentially fraught with danger for budgets.

This paper presents a discussion of the challenges of hybrid environments and attempting to use multiple kinds of platforms for a single workload. With broad knowledge of what traditional HPC workloads and environments look like, what cloud workloads and environments look like, and what pieces of each are most important and problematic, we believe we can take HPC to the Clouds Above!

Acknowledgements

Sandia National Laboratories is a multimission laboratory managed and operated by National Technology & Engineering Solutions of Sandia, LLC, a wholly owned subsidiary of Honeywell International Inc., for the U.S. Department of Energy's National Nuclear Security Administration under contract DE-NA0003525.

REFERENCES

[1] M. J. Cordery, B. Austin, H. Wassermann, C. S. Daley, N. J. Wright, S. D. Hammond, and D. Doerfler, "Analysis of cray xc30 performance using trinity-nersc-8 benchmarks and comparison with cray xe6 and ibm bg/q," in *International Workshop on Performance Modeling, Benchmarking and Simulation of High Performance Computer Systems*, pp. 52–72, Springer, 2013.

[2] K. Pedretti, A. J. Younge, S. D. Hammond, J. Laros, M. L. Curry, M. J. Aguilar, R. J. Hoekstra, and R. Brightwell, "Chronicles of astra: challenges and lessons from the first petascale arm supercomputer," in *SC20: Proc. Int. Conference for High Performance Computing, Networking, Storage and Analysis*, 2020.

[3] D. I. S. Agency, "Department of defense cloud computing security requirements guide." https://rmf.org/wp-content/uploads/2018/05/Cloud_Computing_SRG_v1r3.pdf, 2017.

[4] D. M. Batista, N. L. S. da Fonseca, and F. K. Miyazawa, "A set of schedulers for grid networks," in *Proceedings of the 2007 ACM Symposium on Applied Computing*, SAC '07, (New York, NY, USA), p. 209–213, Association for Computing Machinery, 2007.

[5] A. B. Yoo, M. A. Jette, and M. Grondona, "Slurm: Simple linux utility for resource management," in *Workshop on job scheduling strategies for parallel processing*, pp. 44–60, Springer, 2003.

[6] Y. Fan, Z. Lan, P. Rich, W. E. Allcock, M. E. Papka, B. Austin, and D. Paul, "Scheduling beyond cpus for hpc," in *Proceedings of the 28th International Symposium on High-Performance Parallel and Distributed Computing*, pp. 97–108, 2019.

[7] D. H. Ahn, J. Garlick, M. Grondona, D. Lipari, B. Springmeyer, and M. Schulz, "Flux: A next-generation resource management framework for large hpc centers," in *2014 43rd International Conference on Parallel Processing Workshops*, pp. 9–17, IEEE, 2014.

[8] T. Lynn, P. Rosati, A. Lejeune, and V. Emeakaroha, "A preliminary review of enterprise serverless cloud computing (function-as-a-service) platforms," in *2017 IEEE International Conference on Cloud Computing Technology and Science (CloudCom)*, pp. 162–169, 2017.

[9] K. Ousterhout, P. Wendell, M. Zaharia, and I. Stoica, "Sparrow: distributed, low latency scheduling," in *Proceedings of the Twenty-Fourth ACM Symposium on Operating Systems Principles*, pp. 69–84, 2013.

[10] D. Cheng, Y. Chen, X. Zhou, D. Gmach, and D. Milojicic, "Adaptive scheduling of parallel jobs in spark streaming," in *IEEE INFOCOM 2017-IEEE Conference on Computer Communications*, pp. 1–9, IEEE, 2017.

[11] B. Hindman, A. Konwinski, M. Zaharia, A. Ghodsi, A. D. Joseph, R. H. Katz, S. Shenker, and I. Stoica, "Mesos: A platform for fine-grained resource sharing in the data center.," in *NSDI*, vol. 11, pp. 22–22, 2011.

[12] F. Pfeiffer, "A scalable and resilient microservice environment with apache mesos and apache aurora," *SREcon15 Europe*, May 2015.

[13] V. K. Vavilapalli, A. C. Murthy, C. Douglas, S. Agarwal, M. Konar, R. Evans, T. Graves, J. Lowe, H. Shah, S. Seth, *et al.*, "Apache hadoop yarn: Yet another resource negotiator," in *Proceedings of the 4th annual Symposium on Cloud Computing*, pp. 1–16, 2013.

[14] M. Schwarzkopf, A. Konwinski, M. Abd-El-Malek, and J. Wilkes, "Omega: flexible, scalable schedulers for large compute clusters," in *Proceedings of the 8th ACM European Conference on Computer Systems*, pp. 351–364, 2013.

[15] E. A. Brewer, "Kubernetes and the path to cloud native," in *Proceedings of the sixth ACM symposium on cloud computing*, pp. 167–167, 2015.

[16] J. Turnbull, *The Docker Book: Containerization is the new virtualization*. James Turnbull, 2014.

[17] P. A. O'Gorman and J. G. Dwyer, "Using machine learning to parameterize moist convection: Potential for modeling of climate, climate change, and extreme events," *Journal of Advances in Modeling Earth Systems*, vol. 10, no. 10, pp. 2548–2563, 2018.

[18] V. M. Krasnopolsky and M. S. Fox-Rabinovitz, "Complex hybrid models combining deterministic and machine learning components for numerical climate modeling and weather prediction," *Neural Networks*, vol. 19, no. 2, pp. 122–134, 2006.

[19] A. Gupta, P. Faraboschi, F. Gioachin, L. V. Kale, R. Kaufmann, B.-S. Lee, V. March, D. Milojicic, and C. H. Suen, "Evaluating and improving the performance and scheduling of hpc applications in cloud," *IEEE Transactions on Cloud Computing*, vol. 4, no. 3, pp. 307–321, 2014.

[20] Q. He, S. Zhou, B. Kobler, D. Duffy, and T. McGlynn, "Case study for running hpc applications in public clouds," in *Proceedings of the 19th ACM International Symposium on High Performance Distributed Computing*, pp. 395–401, 2010.

[21] M. A. Netto, R. N. Calheiros, E. R. Rodrigues, R. L. Cunha, and R. Buyya, "Hpc cloud for scientific and business applications: taxonomy, vision, and research challenges," *ACM Computing Surveys (CSUR)*, vol. 51, no. 1, pp. 1–29, 2018.

[22] G. Guidi, M. Ellis, A. Buluc, K. Yelick, and D. Culler, "10 years later: Cloud computing is closing the performance gap," *arXiv preprint arXiv:2011.00656*, 2020.

[23] I. Khalil, I. Hababeh, and A. Khreishah, "Secure inter cloud data migration," in *2016 7th International Conference on Information and Communication Systems (ICICS)*, pp. 62–67, IEEE, 2016.

[24] A. S. Sabyasachi, H. M. D. Kabir, A. M. Abdelmoniem, and S. K. Mondal, "A resilient auction framework for deadline-aware jobs in cloud spot market," in *2017 IEEE 36th Symposium on Reliable Distributed Systems (SRDS)*, pp. 247–249, IEEE, 2017.

[25] S. C. University of California, "CROSS Symposium." https://cross.ucsc.edu/symposium/index.html, October 2017.

[26] M. Karo, R. Lagerstrom, M. Kohnke, and C. Albing, "The application level placement scheduler," *Cray User Group*, pp. 1–7, 2006.

[27] N. Desai, "Cobalt: an open source platform for hpc system software research," in *Edinburgh BG/L System Software Workshop*, pp. 803–820, 2005.

[28] S. Q. Lau, S. Campbell, W. T. Kramer, and B. L. Tierney, "Computing protection in open hpc environments," in *Proceedings of the 2006 ACM/IEEE conference on Supercomputing*, pp. 207–es, 2006.

[29] T. Patel, Z. Liu, R. Kettimuthu, P. Rich, W. Allcock, and D. Tiwari, "Job characteristics on large-scale systems: Long-term analysis, quantification and implications," in *2020 SC20: International Conference for High Performance Computing, Networking, Storage and Analysis (SC)*, pp. 1186–1202, IEEE Computer Society, 2020.

[30] G. P. Rodrigo, P.-O. Östberg, E. Elmroth, K. Antypas, R. Gerber, and L. Ramakrishnan, "Towards understanding hpc users and systems: a nersc case study," *Journal of Parallel and Distributed Computing*, vol. 111, pp. 206–221, 2018.

[31] G. Amvrosiadis, J. W. Park, G. R. Ganger, G. A. Gibson, E. Baseman, and N. DeBardeleben, "On the diversity of cluster workloads and its impact on research results," in *2018 {USENIX} Annual Technical Conference ({USENIX}{ATC} 18)*, pp. 533–546, 2018.

[32] N. A. Simakov, J. P. White, R. L. DeLeon, S. M. Gallo, M. D. Jones, J. T. Palmer, B. Plessinger, and T. R. Furlani, "A workload analysis of nsf's innovative hpc resources using xdmod," *arXiv preprint arXiv:1801.04306*, 2018.

[33] C. A. Stewart, T. M. Cockerill, I. Foster, D. Hancock, N. Merchant, E. Skidmore, D. Stanzione, J. Taylor, S. Tuecke, G. Turner, *et al.*, "Jetstream: a self-provisioned, scalable science and engineering cloud environment," in *Proceedings of the 2015 XSEDE Conference: Scientific Advancements Enabled by Enhanced Cyberinfrastructure*, pp. 1–8, 2015.

[34] K. Keahey, J. Anderson, Z. Zhen, P. Riteau, P. Ruth, D. Stanzione, M. Cevik, J. Colleran, H. S. Gunawi, C. Hammock, *et al.*, "Lessons learned from the chameleon testbed," in *2020 {USENIX} Annual Technical Conference ({USENIX}{ATC} 20)*, pp. 219–233, 2020.

[35] D. Duplyakin, R. Ricci, A. Maricq, G. Wong, J. Duerig, E. Eide, L. Stoller, M. Hibler, D. Johnson, K. Webb, *et al.*, "The design and operation of cloudlab," in *2019 {USENIX} Annual Technical Conference ({USENIX}{ATC} 19)*, pp. 1–14, 2019.

[36] B.-N. Hwang, C.-Y. Huang, and C.-L. Yang, "Determinants and their causal relationships affecting the adoption of cloud computing in science and technology institutions," *Innovation*, vol. 18, no. 2, pp. 164–190, 2016.

[37] T. Bicer, D. Chiu, and G. Agrawal, "A framework for data-intensive computing with cloud bursting," in *2011 IEEE international conference on cluster computing*, pp. 169–177, IEEE, 2011.

[38] W. C. Proctor, M. Packard, A. Jamthe, R. Cardone, and J. Stubbs, "Virtualizing the stampede2 supercomputer with applications to hpc in the cloud," in *Proceedings of the Practice and Experience on Advanced Research Computing*, pp. 1–6, ACM, 2018.